BEYOND

☆ ☆ ☆ ☆ ☆ ☆ ☆ ☆ ☆ ☆ ☆ ☆ PERSUASION

SUNY Series on the Presidency: Contemporary Issues
John Kenneth White, editor

BEYOND
PERSUASION

Organizational Efficiency
and
☆ ☆ ☆ ☆ ☆ ☆ ☆ ☆ ☆ ☆ ☆ ☆ Presidential Power

Matthew Robert Kerbel

State University of New York Press

Published by
State University of New York Press, Albany

Printed in the United States of America

For information, address State University of New York Press,
State University Plaza, Albany, N.Y. 12246

Production by Marilyn P. Semerad
Marketing by Theresa A. Swierzowski

Library of Congress Cataloging-in-Publication Data

Kerbel, Matthew Robert, 1958–
Beyond persuasion : organizational efficiency and presidential power / Matthew Robert Kerbel.
p. cm. — (SUNY series on the presidency)
Includes bibliographical references and index.
ISBN 0-7914-0693-8. — ISBN 0-7914-0694-6 (pbk.)
1. Presidents—United States. 2. Executive power—United States.
I. Title. II. Series: SUNY series in the presidency
JK516.K393 1991
353.03'23—dc20 90-42324
CIP

10 9 8 7 6 5 4 3 2 1

This book is dedicated to
my parents, Doris and Sheldon,
and to my sister Susan

CONTENTS

LIST OF FIGURES

LIST OF TABLES

FOREWORD

When Matt Kerbel first circulated his dissertation prospectus to those of us who were on his Ph.D. committee at the University of Michigan, we were fascinated by the topic and approach and also concerned that the project might be too big an undertaking for a doctoral dissertation. Presidential power, after all, is one of the most important and elusive subjects our discipline considers. It is hard to study at all, and especially difficult to penetrate using systematic, quantitative methods. In the end, Kerbel succeeded in producing a rather unique piece of work that can serve as an important building block for scholars intent on better solving the mysteries of presidential influence.

Beyond Persuasion examines the dynamics of presidential power in a novel way. It sheds new light on an important substantive issue and also pushes forward our mastery of ways to study presidential power. It is based on a systematic study of the components of presidential power, examining what happens when presidents actually wield power.

The book relies primarily on data collected from cases of policy success and failure in the Carter and Reagan administrations, with emphasis on the cases and not on the administrations. The results are generalizable to other administrations. Kerbel looks for, and finds, the similarities that exist in the context of presidential triumphs and also in cases where presidents are far less than triumphant.

This project employs a unique and systematic coding of media accounts of presidential policy successes and failures, supplemented by interviews with key administration officials and with members of the White House press corps. The result is an insightful contribution to the field. Kerbel shows that policy successes (and failures) in the very different administrations of Carter and Reagan had much in common, and indicates that personal factors in the successful exercise of presidential power are overstated compared to the import of what he calls the "organizational components" of power.

This book should touch off a lively debate in the field. And the method developed means that others can easily follow up on what is reported here. They can replicate or fail to replicate Kerbel's findings on the similarities that exist when presidents exercise power effectively, regardless of the overall ratio of any given president's successes to failures. They can modify Kerbel's approach as necessary in an attempt to answer questions raised by critiques of this exploratory work and to answer questions not addressed in the text. And they can compare findings using Kerbel's approach to those uncovered using other innovative approaches. *Beyond Persuasion,* then, does what a good academic book should do — and it has the added advantage of a lively style, peppered with anecdotes, to enhance the pleasure of grasping its basic message.

JOEL D. ABERBACH
University of
California, Los Angeles

ACKNOWLEDGMENTS

It would be far too difficult to mention all the people who have contributed to this project through their constructive criticism, guidance, and support. But, I would like to acknowledge those who donated greatly to the development of this study at the outset, most notably Joel Aberbach, Michael Traugott, and the late Jack Walker. I am grateful to Mark Peterson, Phil Henderson, and Gary King for their comments on portions of the manuscript, as I am to the Inter-University Consortium for Political and Social Research in Ann Arbor, Michigan, for the methodological training I received there. I am indebted to John White for his superb editorial guidance, to Peggy Gifford and Dana Foote at SUNY for helping turn a manuscript into a book, and to Anne Bowdin, Susan Burns, and Margie Rice at Villanova University for bearing with me through numerous requests for updated manuscript copies. Finally, to Adrienne Adler, who selflessly gave her love, support, and wisdom, a simple thank-you is hardly enough. Her influence may be felt on every page.

INTRODUCTION

It's hard to get people to stop eating chocolate pudding.

But when former President Ford advised participants at a conference I attended some time ago that lunch should be abbreviated in order to keep the proceedings from running late, half-eaten desserts were the norm as people immediately streamed out of the dining room. As any chocolate lover would admit, it would have been the preference of many of us to linger for awhile; indeed, it is quite likely that had I or some other less honored guest made the request, the exodus would have been less instantaneous. But, almost immediately after the president urged us to move, lunch was over. It was, I thought, a clear case of the exercise of raw power.

It was also an unusual case because the impetus for our actions was so easy to observe. For those of us in attendance who acted against our preferences by leaving the lunchroom when we did, it was fairly easy to identify President Ford's request as the stimulus that prompted us to do so. There was an observable time lag between the request and the response, there was no competing catalyst to influence our behavior, and without the presidential announcement it is safe to assume that lunch would have continued. Life beyond the conference room is rarely so clear-cut, and life in Washington, where the exercise of presidential power has implications far beyond dessert, can be downright confusing.

This book will delve into that confusion. Its objective is to understand systematically the components of presidential power, of what happens in particular instances when presidents are understood to wield power. A broad and complex but endlessly fascinating subject, power as it is used in the White House has long eluded rigorous, systematic understanding. Indeed, even finding a consensual definition of the word has been an elusive undertaking. In what follows I offer a new way to approach one understanding of the concept of power, in the hope that the findings presented may serve as a framework for further study. Before beginning, it is important to clarify a few terms.

POWER, INFLUENCE, AUTHORITY, AND LEGITIMACY

The presidential literature is vague and inconclusive when it comes to conceptualizing power and associated ideas. Partly because the terms themselves are vague, there may be a tendency to confuse power with related concepts (such as influence, authority, and legitimacy) or with the objectives toward which it is employed (such as success and effectiveness). To minimize such confusion here, I will attempt to provide a framework for understanding the way the term *power* is used.

Passerin D'Entreves distinguishes between "might" and "power" in a manner parallel to the way I differentiate "power" from "power*s*." What Passerin D'Entreves calls *might* is power in raw form: the state as force, what Weber called *macht*. Although it need not be violent or forceful, the emphasis is on the effect, invariably supplanting one's will on another "regardless of the means used and in spite of any resistance."[1]

But if the means are not forceful—and Neustadt tells us that the president can barely command, no less impose — then "power" is properly seen as one form of influence, as Dahl's individual who can somehow move others to do things they might not otherwise have done.[2] The term *influence* is relativistic: to exercise influence requires ability relative to other persons, and to measure influence requires understanding the dynamics between individuals. Seen as a form of influence, power, too, is a relative term.

It also is dynamic, not so much an entity but a set of interactions, to be understood relative to those who exercise it and in the context in which they play their roles. An important component of that context is the institutional position that gives the power wielder a platform from which to operate, or to rule in the Weberian sense. Passerin D'Entreves uses the term *power* to describe this situation of "force qualified by law,"[3] but his emphasis on legality brings it closer to what I like to call *powers,* in the same sense that Corwin understands power as a function of the president's roles.[4] Power*s* are more closely related to authority than to *macht:* they are formal privileges, rights, or trappings, legal or institutional in nature, which contribute to the influence an individual might wield but that, as Hale points out, are fully transferable to subsequent officeholders.[5] Because he is president, an individual may be widely recognized to be in a position to mobilize the army, invite senators to state dinners, or veto legislation, and he may use these to wield power in the sense that he is the holder of these resources and they are desired by those he seeks to influence. At the end of his term, by institutional design, his successor inherits these formal powers—with no instructions regarding what he can or will do with them.

Closely linked to authority is legitimacy, the acceptance by others that the powerful individual's actions are valid. One may see legitimacy as justification for authority (following Passerin D'Entreves, who argues that such justification cannot be found in force or authority alone), or as a form of nontransferrable personal authority.[6] With authority, it rounds out the context in which the president or any power wielder may operate.

A long tradition in presidential scholarship treats power as authority rather than influence. The perspectives that I place in this category are largely historical analyses that focus on presidential "interpretation" of the office, and legal-constitutional approaches to presidential power.[7] Neustadt's work *Presidential Power,* of course, is not among them; rather, Neustadt looks at presidential actions, essentially how the president wields influence given his particular abilities.[8] By detailing power in this fashion, less attention is paid to the context in which power is wielded—that is, to authority and the influence of other actors. Of course, focus is necessary, but there are risks; as Hale observes,

> To define and measure presidential power in terms of (the president's) ability to make choices and decisions, initiate proposals and veto legislation is to ignore the organization of authority in political and economic institutions. . . . In addition, it ignores the exercise of influence and power of other policy elites in and out of government in limiting the scope of initiation, defining the issues, controlling the agenda, implementing and administrating policy programs, or, in other words, in determining policy results.[9]

The danger is to see power in isolation and in the process to lose sight of the proverbial forest. As a hedge against this, although this work examines presidential behavior, it does so in the context in which the president operates. Whereas it shares with Neustadt the presidential vantage point as its main perspective, other policy actors play more than simply a supporting role. One central premise of this project is that the perceptions of those around the president regarding how the president behaves will influence their response toward him — and, in turn, the results he achieves. Staffers are viewed not as extensions of the president, but as autonomous actors with different agendas whom the president must somehow influence or maneuver. The views and reactions of others can affect the legitimacy and authority of the president and, in so doing, influence the context in which he tries to wield power. Their perceptions are given prominence in this study.

This is made possible in part because I regard power not as an end in itself but as a means to a specific objective: advancing the domestic policy agenda.[10] The reasons for selecting this objective are detailed in Chapter 2. When viewed as a means to something else, power may be no easier to identify, but the intent of power may be more clearly outlined. Thus, I speak more in terms of presidential *success* and presidential *effectiveness* than in terms of presidential power. This is because the things I *observe* are the objectives to which power may be applied. Given an operational definition of success, which I discuss in the first chapter, it is an uncomplicated exercise to identify instances in which the president has been effective. The behaviors I examine are those resources employed by the president during routine interaction with other members of the Washington policy community, for the purpose of attaining the objectives that constitute some presidential "success." These resources are the correlates of power, used toward specific ends in concert with other actors who of course have resources of their own. When I speak of success or effectiveness as visible objectives of power, I use the terms in this light.

PERSONAL VS. INSTITUTIONAL

Placing the exercise of presidential power in the context in which it occurs and connecting it with specific objectives frees us to examine more than the president's persuasive ability. It allows for further study of the president's particular vantage point and the contribution of what I call *institutional factors* — such as organizational efficiency within the White House — to presidential success. I intentionally differentiate institutional items from personal ones to tease out the factors contributing to power that originate with the president himself, such as tendencies toward flexibility and the inclination to grant access to others, from those inherent in the institutional presidency. In so doing, I create two categories that at best are loosely distinguished from each other (could not, for instance, a president be flexible with others in the White House?). Obviously, given the overlap between personal and institutional factors, the distinctions are not meant to be drawn with a heavy pen.

There is an important corollary to this. To further our understanding of power, I have attempted to break it down into its possible component parts, or presidential resources, in order to study each individually. As a consequence, a certain artificiality exists, as well, in some of the distinctions made among resources. Presidential favor giving, for instance, is studied separately from the use of pressure, although obviously favors may be employed to put pressure on someone. Communication within the executive branch is discussed as an element of organizational efficiency, but access between president and presidential appointees, which obviously makes some communication possible, is addressed independently. In Chapter 7, I endeavor to put the resources together in a model that begins to address the relative importance of the individual items discussed in the first six chapters.

METHOD

The method employed in this study is discussed in detail in Chapter 2. Still, a couple of opening comments are in order. This book is offered as an empirical exploration of presidential power; it is designed to serve as an initial attempt to identify patterns of activity that are consistent to presidents when they are successful, and to determine the relative importance of these behaviors both to each other and to circumstantial forces. The result should be a preliminary statement of what has some impact on presidential success — and what does not — based on careful observation of what *has* mattered at specific times over a twenty-year period.

In this regard, this project is intended to address the often-heard call for systematic research on important presidential questions. Most recently, the bid was made by King and Ragsdale:

> Presidential research is at a stage analogous to that at which the discipline of economics found itself in the 1950s and the study of the U.S. Congress found itself in the 1960s. Anecdotes and unsystematic information abound. The key questions of measurement and systematic description have not been answered, and explanation has been attempted with only uneven success. . . . [T]he general paucity of systematic studies may reflect the common misperception that, because only one person is president at a time, statistical analyses are not possible. . . . Once we refocus theoretical attention on the plural presidency, the N = 1 problem vanishes, and a wealth of meaningful data appear.[11]

The analysis focuses on policy cases comparable as presidential domestic policy initiatives that all ended in what I will define as success or failure. At this level, it is possible to explore commonalities across administrations. To illustrate the findings, much attention will be paid to the experiences of two presidents—Carter and Reagan—who are interesting because of the certain similar conditions under which they entered the White House and because of the different results they initially achieved. The two former governors campaigned as outsiders who would clean up the mess in Washington, as media candidates in a time of diminished party control who looked to direct popular support for election, as individuals eager to place their imprint on government policy. In their respective first years, Carter met with limited success; Reagan, with great triumphs. The contrasts between these experiences as illuminated by the data will help illustrate some of the more interesting findings of this work. But consider that, despite popular impression and post-hoc evaluation, *both* Carter and Reagan experienced success and failure, and as we will see, striking similarities exist in the context of their triumphs—and in those of presidents dating back to LBJ. We can explore these similarities by keeping the analysis at the level of the policy case.

Quite naturally, there are problems. The data used to support the observations made in the following pages are at best suggestive and cannot be regarded as absolute or definitive. They are meant to be illustrative of a complex and important phenomenon, suggesting directions for further work, offering support for assumptions rather than proof for theories. My intention is to illuminate, not to predict.

ONE

The President and the Rabbit

Some years back, the following news item seemed to typify for many people the shortcomings of an entire administration:

> WASHINGTON, Aug. 29 (AP) — A "killer rabbit" penetrated Secret Service security and attacked President Carter on a recent trip to Plains, Ga., according to White House staff members who said that the President beat back the animal with a canoe paddle. The rabbit, which the President later guessed was fleeing in panic from some predator, reportedly swam towards a canoe from which Mr. Carter was fishing in a pond. It was said to have been hissing menacingly, its teeth flashing and its nostrils flared, and making straight for the President. Mr. Carter was not injured, and reports are unclear about what became of the rabbit.[1]

How the mighty had fallen. Once hailed as a man of the people, as the outsider who would straighten things up in Washington, Jimmy Carter was mocked nationally for what amounted to a close encounter with a bunny. The absurdity of the situation was not lost on the press or the public. How else could one react to the image of the president "swinging for his life,"[2] in the tongue-in-cheek words of a White House staff member, against the advances of a small creature that normally doesn't swim, no less kill.

Everyone is entitled to embarrassing moments and misunderstandings. But, the "killer rabbit" incident also symbolized the apparent failings of a president who to many was seen as incapable, weak, and even inept. It is common for people to pin global labels on presidents, to assess their competence and achievements in generic fashion. It is also misleading. Although a president may accomplish much of what he sets out to do, or very little, or attain only key goals, it is hardly the case that any president is *entirely* inept and unsuccessful. Likewise, a chief executive remembered as "great" or "strong" is not someone who got *everything* he wanted. No one gets everything he or she wants, and no one is a complete failure, images conjured up by killer rabbits notwithstanding. Our tendency to generalize about entire administrations distorts this.

The results a president gets are attributable, along with various circumstantial factors, to how he exercises power in office. If *every* president gets *some* of what he wants, it may be reasonable to assume that every president finds the right configuration for the levers of power at least some of the time. Perhaps the presidents we remember as "great" manage to do it more often or with greater impact. This is still quite different than saying they do it *all* the time, or saying an "incompetent" president couldn't do it at all. I raise the point because it is all too easy to obscure the already complex — but critical — study of presidential power by choosing to view it as something constant to or characteristic of the president. We may rank our presidents by "greatness," as scholars and journalists are wont to do, but the list will not help us understand just what that intangible quality is, even if we agree without dissent that FDR had "more" of it than did Millard Fillmore. Indeed, it might even complicate things by leading us to a mindset in which we feel it is appropriate to gloss over unsuccessful experiences encountered by even those presidents fortunate enough to head the list of America's top forty.

It is one thing to determine that a particular president was more powerful than another, or, for that matter, stronger, better, or more effective. It is entirely different, but quite important, to figure out what constitutes effective use of the office — in short, to understand the mechanics of presidential power. On this critical point our knowledge is sadly lacking. Perhaps because the subject of power seems so inextricably intertwined with the doings of the person who wields it, we have set our sights on the power wielder to understand it. From here, it is a simple matter to confuse power with the person and focus on the individual rather than the tools used. But in so doing we have clouded our understanding of presidential power by drawing upon a model that places a premium on the president's personality. This has enabled us to treat the subject in idiosyncratic fashion, and to rely on anecdotal accounts of presidential doings as evidence of the way presidential power is wielded. The result has been no less than an entirely inadequate diagnosis of power as it operates *in the office,* as attention is directed away from a richer understanding of the mechanics of exercising power—the tools that enable the president to maximize his potential.

By tools, I do not mean the negative constitutional checks that the president may employ by virtue of his official position, but resources that provide him with the potential to move and motivate others. Indeed, to regard power as emanating from a set of tools is to treat the subject as something that exists over time, across administrations, as exercised by different individuals. The personal model of power defies longitudinal analysis because of its reliance on individual characteristics. But, tools remain for others to employ, for new occupants of the office to learn. They are transferrable, at least to the extent that they remain for new chief executives to master. If one president maximizes power through the use of favors or by refining the operation of the institutional presidency, why, then, can't all presidents do so?

Naturally, it is hard to make general empirical statements about the operation of power that will apply to many events occurring in multiple administrations. Perhaps this is why previous works have failed to do so. If power is aptly described as a machine with levers, as was suggested a moment ago, why should we believe they are the same levers over time, no less adjusted the same way for each presidential triumph? Power is the most fleeting and variable of qualities; it will require great care and some imagination to search for common threads in the ways in which it is exercised at different times.

That is the purpose of this book: to search for the elements typical of that most elusive but important of entities, presidential power. The levers of power probably are adjusted differently from moment to moment; one would anticipate a large number of possible combinations of presidential actions and circumstantial factors together could yield a particular result. It is still possible that *some* levers are curiously set the same way time after time. This work attempts to sort through the myriad actions that occur when presidents exercise power to hunt for such common ground.

I start by assuming that there are central tendencies to the exercise of power, things that increase the likelihood it will be employed effectively despite the fact that they may be obscured by the seemingly helter-skelter activities meeting the eye of the observer. Viewing power in use is a bit like watching the game of Monopoly. In Monopoly, players attempt to generate leverage over other players—something akin to the use of power—through the acquisition of money and property. There is no singular way to win the game, no strategy that will always work. Outcomes appear to be a function of chance, or trial and error; even a carefully considered game plan may fall by the wayside if poor luck or the actions of other players intercede.

Still, some elements may be common to numerous strategies that occur more often than not when the game is won, and so may be seen as being characteristic of the outcome, regardless of the way the dice roll or the number of trips you take to jail. Such things as early property development, a favorable ratio of return to investment, and specific bidding behaviors have been posited as factors likely to enhance one's chances of winning at Monopoly, as items that together with chance and circumstance will move the player toward a favorable outcome.[3] If for a moment we accept that the same may be true of presidential power, we open the possibility that it may be studied as a patterned set of characteristics, not simply as the random actions of a particular president that are ostensibly unrelated to the behavior of a different president at another time, or, for that matter, to the behavior of the same president at another time. In this analysis, I will also speak of likelihoods rather than absolutes, in an attempt to identify presidential actions that occur with great frequency when power is effectively exercised by several presidents on multiple occasions.

To say this is to assert that power per se is an entity distinct from the peculiarities of a given event, or at least that power as such has set characteristics, capable of being identified in numerous and diverse circumstances. This assertion easily can be taken too far, and it is not my purpose to suggest that something as complex as the exercise of power can or should be divorced from the specifics of the setting in which it occurs. Rather, it is to suggest that certain actions are more likely to be exhibited when presidents are said to be powerful, that such is not coincidental, and that as actions and not circumstances, they are typical of the quality scholars are inclined to call power. Although presidential behavior may be understood in the context of specific, isolated events, I will attempt to reach beyond this and make a statement about the nature of power itself, in the belief that it is far more interesting and potentially more useful to explore reasons why *presidents* succeed and fail, than why a particular president may succeed at a given time.

The focus will be on instances in several administrations in which we can assume that presidential power was exercised, sometimes effectively and sometimes not, in an effort to attain policy goals. As there is variability to what all presidents can achieve, it is reasonable to examine a variety of events within as well as between administrations, some presidential accomplishments and others presidential frustrations, for clues to what worked and what did not. Viewing power as a quality that will vary over the course of an administration, rather than thinking of presidents as being singularly powerful or not powerful during their tenure, will enable us to understand power as the fluid entity it is.

To do this, we need to agree on a definition of power. We can rely on the guidance of convention to establish a working understanding of an admittedly broad concept. Traditionally, presidential power was seen as a function of the office, and the various constitutionally derived roles its occupant could play.[4] Thus, the president could be understood to exercise power differently as commander-in-chief than as chief of state, although the dissimilarities displayed here are better understood to stem from the prerogatives or power*s* of the office than from any particular actions taken by its occupant. Over a generation ago, Richard Neustadt departed from this approach and addressed presidential power as a largely personal phenomenon, originating with the actions the president brought to bear on others in the Washington policy community in the effort to get them to follow his lead.[5]

This view of power brings into play the president's ability to convince others that his interests are their interests, especially if this is not actually the case.[6] Not surprisingly, persuasion plays a central role in what amounts to a large-scale presidential sales job, aimed at convincing others that the president's way is the right way. Neustadt addresses the particulars of Washington that contribute to the effort, although this understanding of power is largely a modified version of Robert Dahl's approach, refined and tailored to apply to conditions in force in the Oval Office. Essentially, Dahl tells us that we can recognize power in cases where an individual utilizes some resource or resources available to him to move some other individual or individuals toward his position.[7] Following Neustadt, I employ a definition of power that accepts this principle, although, in contrast to the personal model of power, I hold open the possibility that effective organization of the executive branch may combine with personal "resources" to contribute to the effort.

A resource is any quantity available to the president in his attempt to move others. This broad understanding allows an eclectic variety of behaviors and prerogatives to be studied together. In the pages that follow, I will explore the possibility that presidential power derives from a host of items ranging from tangible favors, to nebulous individual characteristics such as charm and flexibility, to the personal realm of access to the president, to the institutional advantages provided by organizational efficiency in the White House.[8] The composition of specific resources should become clear shortly, when I address the hypothetical use of each by the president, but suffice it to say that the list is extensive and wide-ranging. This is a patchwork, but one that allows for the exploration of a full range of items that may contribute to the exercise of presidential power.

Simply having resources is of marginal value, except to provide the president with a variety of options to employ as power. In their dormant state, the group of resources available for use by the president is what Dahl calls the power base, the starting point for the exercise of power. As "exercise" implies action, it is by using the resources constituting the base that the president or any power wielder tries to generate a response from others. Such actions, or what Dahl calls the *power means*,[9] stem from decisions about which resources to use and how to use them. So, it is possible for the president to offer or not to offer favors, let's say, in exchange for political support. Whether he does so, and how his actions are received, should influence the nature of the support he generates. The exercise of power, then, is predicated on both the existence of resources and the means to use them effectively. The president first must have things to give if he seeks to employ favors in return for political support, but he also must be inclined to use them if they are available and find a way to employ them effectively. At the juncture between knowing which buttons to press and doing so effectively, power is both science and art. Our efforts will focus on discovering the buttons, on uncovering patterns in the way resources are used during instances of presidential effectiveness. As we will see, although presidential resources are not unlimited, neither are they scarce. But, knowing which ones to employ takes skill, and doing so effectively remains the job of the political artist.

By including organization as a resource, I implicitly suggest that the exercise of presidential power includes more than the interpersonal factors to which Neustadt gives great currency. While acknowledging the size and scope of the institutional presidency, Neustadt chose to base his analysis of power on individual performance. Thus, he stated " 'Presidential' on the title page means nothing but the President. 'Power' means *his* influence."[10] Whereas we tend to think of powerful presidents as powerful individuals, it is limiting to proceed as though effectiveness derives from the actions of a single person. When journalists wrote of the policy accomplishments that came out of the early days of the Reagan administration, they often pinned credit on Reagan *and his team*. The relationship they shared was described in terms of its efficiency, as the White House staff was said to work well because goals were clearly defined, accepted, and enacted more or less harmoniously by the principle players. The effect was to generate vital support by enhancing the administration's working relationship with Congress or, if you will, to bolster the president's power.

Interpersonal resources that define persuasiveness will also be thoroughly considered; the purpose here is not to contradict Neustadt, but to build upon his work while developing an empirical framework for the study of power.[11] So, instances in which presidential pressure is applied, threats are made, favors are offered, and the like, will be given careful consideration. My intention is to consider the relationship between a wide array of resources and legislative outcomes, and in so doing to expand the prevalent personal model of presidential power to embrace both its personal and organizational components. Indeed, we will see that both persuasion and organizational efficiency are related to presidential effectiveness over time and across administrations.

At the same time, some personal characteristics of the president are not factors in the power game. For instance, despite what the personal model of power might lead us to believe and contrary to what we may assume to be the case from a casual reading of the first Reagan term, presidential charm and charisma are of limited utility to the exercise of power. We will see that, although Ronald Reagan's charismatic way was not lost on others in the Washington community, it alone was not enough to help steer him from defeat. Likewise, other less enchanting chief executives accomplished much without a warm smile and endearing quips. It is all too easy to overstate the importance of charm when employing a model of power that emphasizes the individual to the exclusion of the tools used.

Identifying specific purposes for which power is exercised is critical to the development of the model. To what end is presidential power employed? Neustadt spoke of power in its own terms, as something of value to the president that he should strive always to maximize.[12] Implicitly, he saw the powerful president as a good president, and the acquisition of power more an end in itself than a means to an end. As a result, power is not treated in the context of what its exercise could bring about, but as something the president should amass. Not surprisingly, power becomes inseparably braided with the person who exercises it. In this study, the means to power are rooted in some of the ends it may achieve, in moving Congress and the executive branch toward specific objectives. This will enable us to view the subject with a wider lens, to look at power from multiple perspectives, both interpersonal and institutional, in the effort to enhance our understanding of what it is and how it works. When I claim, for instance, that the place of Reagan's charm has been overstated, I mean to suggest that it has been overstated in the context of domestic policy endeavors he attempted to get through Congress. These, as much as anything, were among Reagan's most salient objectives as he, like most presidents, endeavored to use his power to make his mark on American public policy.

As an empirical analysis of presidential power, this project focuses on actual events in order to understand what really happened when a given president exercised power effectively. Where Neustadt was primarily concerned with the potential exercise of power, with what the president could or should do if he wanted to be powerful, my objective is to begin to understand what actually has worked and what has not.

I examine only domestic policy initiatives,[13] speaking of them in the simple shorthand of success and failure. A policy "success" is the realization, often by an act or set of actions by the legislature, of a policy goal previously sought by the president in both rhetoric and actions. In other words, it is something to which the president committed himself well beyond simple lip service. A "failure," for my purposes, occurs when comparable presidential attention yields results adverse to the president's stated position or no results at all. The terms, as they are used here, do not apply to the impact of a given policy once it is realized, nor are they intended to be pejorative in any respect. They are used as a simple way to distinguish presidential victory from defeat.

The task is to refine our understanding of presidential power by examining it in vivo, to connect the means of power to its ends and examine a sample of instances when the means were brought to bear on actual objectives. It is to define better those aspects of power that derive from the person and distinguish them from organizational factors. Ultimately, it is to make a rudimentary but important judgment about *how much* a given resource contributes to presidential power relative to all other resources available to a president, for multiple cases of success over a period of twenty years.

But, understanding presidential power is more complicated than this simple statement makes it seem. Even when we can identify instances when a president successfully accomplishes a policy goal, and distinguish them from occasions when he does not, we remain hard pressed to isolate the combination of factors and forces that forged the outcome. How, for instance, do we discriminate behavior from context? How much of a particular triumph may be attributed to a president's actions in office, as opposed to the opportunities afforded by circumstance? Power implies behavior; favorable outcomes produced without action are better understood as products of happenstance or even luck. Yet, circumstances will constrain some behaviors and facilitate others, potentially affecting the president's ability to wield power in pursuit of his goals. We will need to give this careful consideration.

Furthermore, the resources a president may draw upon are

many. Some will advance his objectives, but others will have no effect or even may be detrimental. To understand power in terms of resources requires a direct connection between presidential actions and favorable results, a link not likely to be apparent for all the things the president does. The president may cajole others, offer them favors, kill them with kindness, flatter them with charm, or dazzle them with expertise. In the end, he may get them to see things his way. He may not stop to discriminate between effective and ineffective actions; for that matter, he may believe that a little bit of everything he did contributed to the outcome. And, maybe it did. It is equally reasonable if not more cautious to assume that some actions ultimately mattered more. Of course, it is quite another thing to identify those actions and relate them to results. Where the connections are not obvious, we will hunt for them. Where information is lacking, we will rely on careful extrapolation. In so doing, we stand to better our understanding of what constitutes presidential power.

In Chapter 2, I discuss in greater detail how the study reported here was conducted and, using two case studies, identify the resources that will be considered for their contributions to presidential effectiveness. Chapters 3 and 4 will be devoted to systematic analysis of the resources a president may use to persuade others, and their relationship to the results he achieves.

In Chapter 5, I will address the institutional face of power, by considering organizational efficiency as a factor contributing to policy success. Congressional access to the president and the White House will be discussed in Chapter 6 as an item of some importance to policy outcomes, and one that the president has much leeway to control. Three resources were found to be of limited utility in shaping legislative outcomes: competence, charisma, and hard work. These, too, will be addressed in Chapter 6. Despite what conventional wisdom tells us about the importance of being able and working hard, and despite what the personal model of power might lead us to believe about the importance of charm, no relationship was found between these items and successful policy outcomes.

Chapter 7 presents a multivariate model for the exercise of power, in a preliminary effort to make relative statements about the importance of factors heretofore discussed and in an attempt to weigh the overall importance of power with respect to circumstance or situation to the outcome of a policy event. General conclusions about the exercise of presidential power will be discussed in Chapter 8. Observations about the exercise of power during the first months of the Bush administration will be considered in a postscript.

weigh the overall importance of power with respect to other circumstances or situation to the outcome of a policy event. Our final conclusion about the exercise of presidential power will be discussed in Chapter 6. Observations about the exercise of power during the first months of the Bush administration will be considered in a postscript.

TWO

Policy Outcomes: Power and Context

From what has been said so far, presidential power seems not only nebulous, but terribly idiosyncratic, a peculiar set of behaviors that mesh at a given time with specific circumstances to yield a particular result. And, it is true that the manner in which a president exercises power will derive in part from how the individual is apt to behave in office at a given moment. This is especially likely in an office like the American presidency, so highly touted as a ''personal branch'' of government that responds to the actions of its occupant like a seismograph to an earthquake. It is *not* clear, however, that the exercise of power is entirely idiosyncratic, or for that matter even predominantly so. If we can unearth behavioral similarities applicable to multiple instances of presidential success covering many years and several administrations, we can begin to speak in systematic fashion about the characteristics of presidential power in that period. If we can further identify the relative lack of those behaviors during instances when the same presidents failed to effect their objectives, we can begin to speak of actions exclusive to power.

To do so, it must first be possible to identify presidential behavior, evaluate it, and connect it with specific policy outcomes. This means being able to identify the resources the president uses to promote the objectives he wishes to achieve with his power. More precisely, it means exploring the impression made by the president on the principle actors he needs to mobilize in order to realize his objectives. As power is assumed here to be used for the sole purpose of the advancement of domestic legislation, key individuals will most likely be affiliated with Congress or the executive branch. So, in reality, *their perceptions* of presidential behavior are of primary interest.

Lest this seem to obfuscate an already obscure topic, consider that it may be as easy if not easier to garner personal perceptions of the president from the principle players than to generate an abstract and entirely impartial understanding of how the president uses his resources. To demonstrate this, think about the concept of charm, a resource of potential value to the process of persuasion. One could define charm, perhaps agreeing on a set of characteristics it encompasses. But, identifying these characteristics in presidential behavior would necessarily require judgment; what is charming to one person may be revolting to another. The dictionary tells only that charm is "a trait that fascinates, allures, or delights." Like pornography, it may be different things to different people, although we're likely to know it right away when we see it.

This holds for the people who interacted with the president, to whom he directed his charm if he indeed employed it at all. One need only to find their responses to him to determine if the resource was called into service. If they *believed* the president drew upon his charm, then the net effect was the use of that resource, regardless of what an independent measure of charm might suggest. In essence, the researcher's interpretation is irrelevant, because he was not the focus of a president's attempt to wield power within the policy community. The reality of power rests with the perceptions of those the president needs to reach. Only if they believe him to be powerful will they be moved. The data employed here reflect this perspective.

THE DATA

The challenge, then, is not to objectify presidential behavior, but to record it accurately as it is witnessed by participants in the policy process. Ideally, each time a policy actor notes or mentions a particular presidential behavior in the context of a policy pursuit, it should be recorded. Short of mind reading, there are two ways to gather this type of information: by speaking to the principles, and by examining the printed record of events.

Elite interviewing, though it leads one to the source of observations, is a risky procedure to employ for this type of operation. The information desired is precise; if the president twisted a respondent's arm at a White House luncheon, that individual would need to be able to recall the event, link it specifically to the policy the president was trying to attain with his power, and remember how he or she responded. Perhaps with unlimited time to interview, it would be possible to touch on a number of such occurrences. Perhaps if the events at issue had happened within a week or two of the interview, it would be possible for respondents to remember them with some accuracy. In reality, fixed-length interviews are likely to yield coarse responses about past events, and memory decay makes it inconceivable that even the sharpest mind could remember with accuracy and precision events of twenty, ten, five, or even two years ago. And these difficulties say nothing about the problems posed by gaining access to the principles, or of the potential for the respondents' own political needs to color, consciously or otherwise, the content of a response.

The printed record overcomes these problems. Newspapers, periodicals, journals, and the like provide detailed accounts of the daily workings of Washington. They are a standard source for data, but as the data used here are not standard, care should be taken to ensure that the printed record is an appropriate source for this study. The unit of analysis is the mention of a presidential resource by any policy player. Simply by reading the newspaper, it should be apparent that there are numerous mentions of presidential contact with members of Congress, of high-pressure and soft-sell efforts to persuade, of division or harmony within the president's inner circle, and of other items soon to be identified as possible resources used in the exercise of power. They are invariably attributed to a source, so the origin of a given perception may be determined clearly and unambiguously; if an observation is attributed to a particular senator, for example, it is clear that the individual named is the one who made it.

However, the printed record presents the researcher with other difficulties. First, it yields aggregate data. Composite perceptions of presidential resource use may not be used to make statements about individual observations or reactions, nor may they be used to draw specific connections between individual observations and behavior. As a result, it is necessary to make the reasonable assumption that some connection exists between the way, say, members of Congress claim in the aggregate to perceive the president and how they act individually. The objective is to devise a reasonable account of behavior from collective observations.

Second, there is no way to ensure that the set of observations in print is in any way complete. This can be partially checked by relying on multiple media, but there is no way to capture private, unrecorded observations. It is also possible that some presidents faced a more critical press, although many journalists, like David Gergen, claim that standards for presidential coverage are uniformly high: "We [reporters] have a tendency to jump on our presidents too hard; too rarely do we give them the benefit of the doubt; we subject them to standards that no individual could meet; we build them up when they are first elected and portray them as saviors of our system. When we see a flaw, a chink in the armor, we jump all over them."[1] As long as these standards are uniformly enforced, the nature of coverage will not be a factor. If some presidents nonetheless appear to receive harsher treatment, it will not matter as long as the harsh treatment is applicable to the entire presidency, to their successes as well as their failures. Either way, this project focuses on specific mentions of individual resources, which may be positive in nature even if the global tone of coverage is critical.

Overall, journalistic descriptions may be among the more reliable accounts of events. Biographic narratives would have the advantage of the first-person perspective. But, they do not always exist, and when they do, they too may have been influenced by the corrosive effects of time and quite possibly by the self-serving nature of so many personal histories. On this basis, I chose to rely on journalistic accounts, even if they can relate only the perceptions of principle actors *as recorded by* reporters. My primary concern is not for the integrity of what is reported but for the distance an item had to travel from the initial observation to its place in the dataset. In the printed record, observations of presidential resources appear in processed, not raw, form.

In essence, relying on the printed record trades time for distance. Actors make observations and they are recorded within moments, preserved for eternity on microfilm, safe from the dangers of memory decay. However, they are recorded by an agent, and so must travel through the reporter's typewriter before becoming available to the researcher. Finally, the researcher must process observations in the printed record with the aid of a coding scheme. The instrument I used is a rather elaborate one, but it was carefully employed; as a result, intercoder reliability is quite high, as one can see by observing Appendix A. Still, the trade-offs necessitated by resorting to the printed record should be kept in mind and, although it affords the most accurate way to assess how presidential resource use was perceived, care needs to be taken when drawing inferences from the data.

In most instances, we will speak of whether a particular resource was perceived by the observer to have been employed by the president when an observation of that resource was recorded in print. Recalling Dahl's power construct, we may remember that the president is assumed to operate with an array of resources, or a power base, that is dormant until the president draws upon it. An observation of a resource is evidence that it exists in the power base. But, the president may or may not use it. Thus, it is possible for an observer to comment upon the existence of a resource and note either that is was or was not used. Following a meeting with the president, for instance, an observer might note that a form of pressure was applied. Or, she might comment upon the opposite—that the president did not try to persuade her. The former is an instance of what will be called the *use* of a resource, the latter, of the *failure* to use a resource.

Such "nonevents" are indeed captured by reporters and retained in the printed record. Of course, the possible set of such observations is infinite, as people are constantly "not observing" all sorts of things. What interests me are the "nonevents" salient enough to observers to warrant mention, and the manner in which they are distributed across cases of policy success and failure. In theory, successful execution of power rests with the use of resources in an absolute sense, as well as with the way particular resources are employed. We should expect to find successful presidential enterprises peppered heavily with resource use. But, the distinction between heavy and light resource use is arbitrary if approached in isolation. Comparing resources "used" to resources "not used" in both successful and unsuccessful policy endeavors is one way to create an appropriate context for understanding the power means. Successful outcomes should show a higher rate of resource use.

For some resources, the terminology of use is a bit strained. I will speak of the nature of organization in the White House, for instance, where the resource of value is efficiency. If the president is observed to be running an efficient organization, based on criteria to be discussed shortly, it may be said that he is putting the resource to use. Conversely, observations of organizational inefficiency indicate that he is not reaping the possible benefits of being organized; as such, the resource is not being put to use, even though the behavior displayed is not tantamount to, say, a straightforward presidential refusal to offer a favor.

This unconventional approach is necessitated by the complexity of the subject and the difficulty associated with trying to capture systematically the working of power. To visualize better how the data were collected, as well as to develop a more intuitive understanding of what is meant by the use and nonuse of resources, the reader is advised to see Appendix B, which excerpts two articles used for this study, and demonstrates how the content analysis of those articles was performed.

Two original datasets will be used, each composed of perceptions by Washington actors of presidential resources. The primary dataset aggregates such observations for eight salient domestic policy cases during the Carter administration and Ronald Reagan's first term. Most of these cases were of long duration, yielding a sizable number of individual resource mentions.[2] All told, 3,109 mentions of presidential resources were coded from stories about these eight events in the *New York Times*, the *Washington Post*, major periodicals, and the "CBS Evening News." All stories about each event were reviewed in their entirety from the date the president committed himself to pursuing the policy until the moment a final outcome was determined.

Four events were "successes" and four were "failures," these divided evenly between the two administrations. They serve as the point of departure for this analysis of power. Rich in resource mentions, they allow for the observation of power dynamics in two administrations noted for their vastly different administrative styles and policy objectives. Similarities in their respective successes will serve as a springboard for discussion of the common threads of presidential power, those behaviors addressed in Chapter 1 that crop up much more often than not when the Monopoly game is won. Are two presidents as different as Reagan and Carter perceived to be disorganized, on the whole, when they fail, yet well organized when they succeed? Are they perceived to bring the full weight of persuasion to their successful efforts, but something much less than that to their failures? These are the types of preliminary observations that will be made.

Based on the findings of the Carter and Reagan cases, a supplementary dataset will be used to infer how broadly applicable the initial observations may be.[3] Thirteen successes and thirteen failures were randomly selected from a universe of major domestic initiatives of the Johnson, Nixon, and Ford administrations[4] and coded for mentions of resources previously suggested to play a role in the exercise of power. With the help of these data, it will be possible to determine if observations pertinent to the exercise of power in the Carter and Reagan administrations hold for other major domestic policy campaigns since 1964.[5] These data will also be used for a preliminary analysis of the interaction of presidential resources.

A list of the cases used in this study may be found in Appendix C. Two will be examined in detail here to get a feel for how a failure contrasts with a success, and to understand better the nature of the resources to be examined.

EXPLORING DIVERGENT OUTCOMES

Come back in time to 1977.

The new president, barely inaugurated, was hard at work on a comprehensive energy proposal aimed at meeting the long-term needs of a fuel-hungry America. Against a backdrop of accolades from pundits and warm congressional wishes, the chief executive and his agents plunged into battle, eager to take on foreign and domestic oil producers, the federal bureaucracy, and even doubting members of the American public, lest their skepticism about the magnitude of the crisis stand in the way of treating it. The objectives were enormous and the odds were long, but this was war; to the president of the United States, losing the fight against energy dependency would be as destructive to national survival as battlefield defeat.

His choice of an enemy may have been pertinent, but history tells us that President Carter's rhetoric and actions bore little fruit. Shortly after the energy battle was enjoined, a most appropriate combat analogy appeared to be the latter days of Vietnam, as the president found himself fighting on three fronts, taking on the energy crisis itself, a Congress divided over its inclination to wage war, and a public uncertain about the need and purpose for sacrifice. The fanfare of February became the impasse of April and, ultimately, defeat by December.

Now consider what happened four years later.

Another new president, his moving van hardly out of view on Pennsylvania Avenue, began campaigning for unprecedented reductions in the federal budget, seeking to alter radically the spending priorities of a generation. The effort would be equal to the energy battle in scope and controversy, as the president found it necessary to rally Congress and the public behind his initiative. And, to this president, the endeavor would be just as important and far-reaching, as he proclaimed unnecessary government expenditures to be the root cause of America's immediate and long-term economic troubles. Without a doubt, the effort invested by President Reagan and his staff was comparable in intensity to the Carter initiative. Only the outcome was different. By midsummer 1981, champagne toasts in the Oval Office proclaimed a great victory for the young administration's budget initiative. In roughly six month's time, Ronald Reagan realized a domestic policy triumph unmatched in scope by his predecessor.

Why did one "rookie" president succeed whereas another failed? Granted, part of the answer lies in the particular circumstances surrounding each event. But, something interesting may be observed from a different perspective. Beyond situation-specific occurrences and things that can be written off to luck and chance, the different outcomes of these two events may be understood, respectively, as the bitter and sweet fruit of the labors of two chief executives. In the instances discussed here we find two examples—one successful, the other not—of the use of presidential power.

The Carter energy initiative and Reagan budget drive are contextually comparable. Each originated during the "honeymoon" period of a president who came to Washington as a fresh face, after campaigning as an outsider who was prepared to shake things up once settled in Washington. Each addressed an issue earmarked by the president as the biggest problem facing the country at the time. And, as noted, each was ambitious in scope and in its respective challenge to well-enmeshed special interests. I will briefly explore the evolution of each case, and consider environmental and behavioral differences that could explain why Carter's plan ended in frustration whereas Reagan's efforts paid off. In the process, it will be possible to make generalizations about the phenomenon of power and to consider how some of the ways these specific outcomes have been explained may serve as a basis for understanding the workings of power *writ large*.

Carter's Energy Plan: Frustration

In the wake of the Arab oil embargo of the mid-1970s, America had become aware of the possibility that seemingly abundant supplies of low-cost energy may be finite. Against this backdrop, President Carter decided to commit his young administration and the nation to do battle with energy dependency. During a nationally televised address on April 18, 1977, the president outlined to the public the details of the comprehensive energy package his administration was proposing to combat the problem. His tone was somber as he declared, in words borrowed from William James, the "moral equivalent of war" against our energy problems.

In truth, the administration had begun an all-out push for its energy package months before, almost immediately following the inauguration. There was no doubt that Carter had decided to take the political capital afforded him by Congress and the public during his "honeymoon" period, and turn it into an energy program bearing his mark. The quest was ambitious—gas and oil taxes, levies on gas guzzlers, natural gas deregulation, a cabinet-level Energy Department, and the development of alternative energy supplies were only a few of the items proposed—but the president's Democratic party held a majority in both houses of Congress, and his Gallup approval rating was 66 percent in late February.

Through February and March, as Carter prepared the American public for the sacrifices his program would require, James Schlesinger, slated to head the proposed Department of Energy, worked privately on much of the actual legislation the administration would propose. His seclusion ruffled the congressional leadership, many of whom felt they were being precluded from participating in the planning, and John B. Oakes of the *New York Times* was already beginning to question the leadership ability of a president who had been in office barely eight weeks.[6] For his part, Carter acknowledged that the call to sacrifice could hurt him politically. Nonetheless, the president's job approval rating continued to rise steadily, to 71 percent on March 13 and 75 percent on April 8.[7] After the April announcement, the president went to work on two fronts, trying to convince the American public that his dire predictions about future energy reserves were accurate, while drumming up support in Congress. The immediate results were not good. A CBS News/New York Times poll released April 29 revealed that, although a large majority of the public felt confident that Carter could handle the energy situation, most did not believe that it was a crisis. Not surprisingly, given limited public support and the controversial nature of the energy legislation, congressional prospects were questionable. Complaints, now legendary, about Carter's reluctance to enjoin the interpersonal political battle were becoming more commonplace on the Hill. After only several weeks in office, doubts already clouded this legislative centerpiece of the young administration; albeit lightly, the handwriting was appearing on the wall.

When Schlesinger testified before the House Ways and Means Committee on May 17 to answer questions about the energy package, he met with bipartisan reservations. Less than a month later, that committee would kill the three-cent per gallon tax designed to fund mass transit and energy research. For his part, the president began backpedaling on the extent of the public sacrifice he felt the energy program would require, as his Gallup approval rating sank 11 percentage points during the two months after he unveiled his plan. By mid-June, Senate Majority Leader Robert Byrd was publicly castigating a president of his own party for ineffective lobbying,[8] as Carter, to the amazement of many Washington politicians, expressed *his* surprise that the auto and oil lobbies were organized enough to "chip away" at his program.[9]

Nevertheless, under the leadership of Speaker O'Neill, the House on August 5 approved a comprehensive energy bill that was largely intact, save for the watered-down gas tax increase. This happened despite a late-summer survey suggesting that too few people believed America's energy problems were serious enough to provide broad support for the Carter initiative.[10] Indeed, lagging public support was only one of Carter's problems in the Senate, where all the tax provisions included in his program faced a hostile Finance Committee chaired by Senator Russell Long, of oil- and gas-rich Louisiana. On September 26, Carter called on the Senate to "act responsibly" and to "reject narrow, special interest attacks on all segments of the national energy plan."[11] His words were far from effective, as the Senate continued "dismantling" the energy program.[12] On October 5, Senator Abraham Ribicoff, a Connecticut Democrat, called the package "a shambles"[13] and urged Carter to start again with something new.

On the defensive, and facing criticism from leaders of *both* parties, the president inaugurated a campaign-style swing to round up public support for his package. But, by October 19, with his job approval rating down to 59 percent, Carter was forced to take what the Senate would give him—a skeletal energy tax bill that cleared the upper house, 52–35, on Halloween. It bore barely a family resemblance to the proposal Carter put forth with much fanfare when his administration was young, and key differences still remained between the Senate and the House versions. The result was stalemate. On December 12, Walter Cronkite read the death notice: "Conferees got nowhere today on the energy bill, and congressional leaders decided to adjourn for the year after Thursday's sessions. With that, the Carter administration admitted defeat."[14] The next day, Carter conceded that Congress would not pass even the essential outlines of his energy program in 1977. Subsequently, he would call congressional failure to pass his energy legislation the "only major failure" of his first year in office.[15]

Reagan's Budget Proposal: Fruition

Ronald Reagan wasted little time moving to make unprecedented cuts in the federal budget. Arriving in Washington on the crest of an electoral vote landslide that magnified modest popular support, Reagan claimed a mandate for reversing what he saw as decades of wasteful government spending. Nine days after taking the oath of office, the president announced that the budget cuts sought by his administration would be "bigger than anyone has ever attempted,"[16] and he laid out his case in broad terms during a nationally televised address on February 5. The speech met with bipartisan support in Congress, a function of the political climate during the honeymoon period and, no doubt, of efforts by the new president to make friends on the Hill.[17] Public response was not nearly as warm, with protests arising from groups that stood to lose from anticipated cuts in social welfare spending.

Where James Schlesinger labored in the early days of the Carter regime to mold a comprehensive energy plan, David Stockman worked vigilantly on proposing spending reductions during the comparable point in the Reagan administration, ironing out the details of the budget proposal from his vantage point as director of the Office of Management and Budget. Similarly, Reagan followed the public relations approach that had been attempted during the early Carter days, a two-pronged public and congressional relations campaign, initiated in mid-February, to head off growing public opposition to his spending cuts and to work for votes in Congress. It began with the president's February 18 State of the Union address, a speech dedicated almost entirely to his proposed $41.1-billion budget cuts and to related economic matters. Given the dynamics of the honeymoon period, it should not be surprising that the speech was greeted with generally sympathetic public response, tempered by continued stiff opposition from groups that felt threatened.[18] This pattern is analogous to the general sense of confidence placed in Carter's ability to handle the nation's energy problems following the "moral equivalent of war" speech—a feeling that did not extend to oil and gas interests.

Reagan, like his predecessor, found congressional Democrats to be less than united. Only this time, they were the loyal opposition, and their disorganization worked to the benefit of the president. On March 11, the day after Reagan formally submitted his budget to Congress, House Democratic leaders initiated a counteroffensive, vowing to propose an alternative measure designed to preserve many of the social programs sitting precariously under the Reagan budget axe. But, one week later, the Republican majority on the Senate Budget Committee unanimously approved a Republican-backed package that recommended $2.3 billion in cuts above what the president had requested. Disunited, the opposition could not retard the gradual progress of the proposal. Still, things were moving slowly. The president's job approval rating in mid-

March rested at 60 percent in the Gallup poll, several percentage points below Carter's figure after his first two months in office. Then, on March 30, the bullet that almost ended Ronald Reagan's life created a second start for his administration.

As Reagan recovered rapidly from his wound, his legislative team moved swiftly to capitalize on a renewed feeling of good will. A second lobbying blitz was introduced in mid-April. On April 28, with two of three Americans now voicing support for the president, Reagan invoked the spirit of his second honeymoon in a personal appeal for his budget package to a joint session of Congress. The response was tremendous, both during the speech and in the wake of it, as the House began debate on the package. By early May, conservative House Democrats joined with Republicans to give the president his first major victory, rejecting liberal alternatives and adopting the Reagan-endorsed budget proposal. Within a week, the Senate followed suit by approving a comparable package. On May 28, his Gallup approval rating at 68 percent, President Reagan was well on his way to realizing his spending objectives.

Still, the hardest part was yet to come, as the actual budget cuts now had to be made. To this end, David Stockman had a strategy. Employing an obscure budgetary provision called *reconciliation,* he aimed to force Congress to consider the cuts in one lump sum in the respective budget committees of each house, rather than in the decentralized manner that would make it easier for special interests to protect their own turf. It was by no means an easy task; reconciliation was a congressional provision, which Congress had the right to change or suspend, and the stakes were high.

The president responded with another intensive lobbying campaign, at one point accusing congressional Democrats of trying to sabotage the budget.[19] His public approval rating plummeted as the conflict heated up, dropping 9 percentage points in less than one month. But, his efforts were rewarded. An attempt by House Democrats to consider the budget cuts as six separate packages — thus reducing the likelihood that they would be approved — was defeated on June 25. From there, the way was cleared for the House to approve a $32.8-billion package of cuts, which it did the next day, by a 217–211 vote. With the Senate already having approved a comparable package, all that remained was a midsummer conference to iron out the details. By the first of

August, final congressional approval had been granted to over $35 billion in budget cuts, a dramatic reversal of federal spending priorities that the president happily signed into law in mid-August. *Time* magazine assessed the scope of the victory: "Not since the first six months of Franklin Roosevelt's administration has a new President done so much so quickly to change the economic direction of the nation. Reagan not only won 90% of his economic program, but did so with a display of political organization and savvy that left his opponents reeling in disarray."[20] By early September, Reagan's public approval rating stood at 60 percent,[21] exactly where it had been in the early days after he took office, before his "revolution" began.

CONTEXTUAL EXPLANATIONS: BEYOND A PRESIDENT'S CONTROL

Numerous explanations have been offered for why these two presidents met such vastly different fates.[22] In 1977, much was made of Jimmy Carter's posture as a Washington outsider, which accurately described the image and reality of his relationship to the federal establishment. The argument, especially popular with some in the press corps, was that a president with no prior Washington experience lacked the tools necessary to make the establishment respond to his wishes. Put this way, Carter's problem was seen to be situational. By extension, any individual who opens shop in the Oval Office without the prior experience of a Johnson or a Nixon or a Ford starts with the game all but lost. The reasoning is sound, but it is undermined by the Reagan experience, in which the simple fact that the president took office as an outsider (and, for public relations purposes, continued to portray himself as one to the American people) did not preclude him from experiencing unexpected legislative success in the early months of his administration. Some might add that Carter *remained* the outsider in substance and form, whereas Reagan moved quickly to become accepted by the community he continued to chastise publicly. But, that is a matter of behavior, not of circumstance; I will address behavioral specifics shortly.

The first two explanations in Table 2.1 address other circumstantial possibilities for why these two cases ended differently.

Table 2.1. Possible Explanations for Differences in Carter and Reagan First-Year Policy Outcomes

Explanations with Their Origins in Circumstance:

1. Differences in the level of popular support
2. Differences in congressional orientation or makeup

Explanations with Their Origins in Presidential Power:

3. Differences in presidential persuasiveness
4. Differences in efficiency within the White House organization
5. Differences in access between the president and Congress
6. Differences in the availability or use of presidential charm or charisma
7. Differences in technical expertise
8. Differences in effort or initiative

They may also be viewed as general explanations of circumstantial factors that may universally constrain or encourage the effective exercise of power. The first of these suggests that the divergent outcomes of the two initiatives may be linked to differences in popular support. This is a reasonable assertion if we accept the plausible argument that presidential actions and their impact in Washington are circumscribed by the president's prevailing level of support among his national constituency. What the president can accomplish is bounded by the status derived from public prestige, which, as Neustadt compellably argues, will affect the way he is received in the Capital. But note, both Carter and Reagan experienced the downward progression in popular support one would expect to find as the honeymoon wanes.[23] Reagan's approval ratings in the Gallup poll were between 8 and 11 percentage points *lower* than the comparable ratings for Carter during his first spring in office. And, on September 6, 1981, after he had successfully maneuvered his budget plan through Congress, 60 percent of the American public said they approved of the job he was doing as president. On October 19, 1977, with his energy package crumbling, a comparable 59 percent of the public willingly gave a vote of confidence to Carter.[24] Although it is true that Carter had fallen further, it is also true that Reagan had managed to do more with less.

It is quite possible—indeed, intuitive—that popular support could have a hand in influencing the outcome of some presidential initiatives, and this possibility will be explored subsequently.[25] It may also be the case that particular items to which support scores are sensitive contribute independently to the likelihood of presidential achievement.[26] The state of the economy, for instance, could constrain or advance the president's prospects through the impact it has on public confidence in him. Controversial, large-scale events such as Watergate and the Vietnam war may affect not just the president's standing with the public, but his ability to have his way with Congress on unrelated matters. Either possibility is plausible, and consistent with the place of popular support in a democracy.

By the same token, the institutional relationship between Congress and the president may readily influence the likelihood of presidential policy success. In one respect, this may be seen as an ongoing macroevent, a battle for dominance that is a fundamental characteristic of the relationship.[27] Depending upon when the president takes office, he will inherit a Congress either more or less inclined to work with him. Jimmy Carter happened to take office during a period of congressional reassertion following the strong presidencies of Johnson and Nixon and had to work within the constraints pursuant to this while selling his energy package. Ronald Reagan, in turn, became president at a time when some felt the office had overtaken its last occupant, amidst public clamor for a strong leader to fill big shoes. This, coupled with a disorganized Democratic party still in shock after losing control of the White House and the Senate, made possible a resurgence of the executive and enhanced the prospects for enactment of the controversial budget proposal.

The same relationship may be captured by examining the partisan composition of Congress, although when one views sheer numbers rather than institutional orientation, one finds little cause for Carter's energy failure. If anything, a Democratic president should be expected to benefit from a Congress dominated by his partisan counterparts. Ronald Reagan, who could count on a Republican majority only in the Senate, nonetheless prevailed with his budget initiative. If it appears in these instances that the orientation and composition of Congress are working against each other, it should be noted again that all presidents attain some degree of success in office, as the term has been defined here, despite what may be assumed to be a reasonably constant posture vis-à-vis Congress. Macroevents, by definition, change slowly, but within a period of congressional assertion or control by the opposite party, presidents still manage to succeed some of the time. Such conditions may go farther in explaining why some presidents succeed *more often* than others.

The remaining explanations presented in Table 2.1 for why the Carter and Reagan honeymoon initiatives met such different fates will also be applied to the major domestic policy initiatives to be examined here, undertaken by presidents from LBJ to Reagan, in an effort to determine which factors are related to successful outcomes. Although not exhaustive, the list of possible items contributing to effectiveness is wide-ranging and diverse. As the focus of this work is power, attention will be paid predominantly to behavioral tenets of policy success, illustrated as they pertain to the Carter and Reagan honeymoon initiatives by items 3 through 8 in Table 2.1.

POWER EXPLANATIONS: PRESIDENTS AND THEIR ORGANIZATIONS

Power resources are things the president can control. Unlike circumstantial factors, their use is a matter of choice or skill. Where the president can do nothing about the composition of Congress or his immediate pool of popular support, he can choose to exercise any number of prerogatives from bargaining to organizing to try to get his way.

He may bring to bear manifold resources to employ what Neustadt calls *persuasion* in dealing with others, especially Congress. Persuasion may be the most straightforward exercise one can attempt in the effort to move others closer to one's position, but, like the concept of power itself, persuasion is easier to recognize than to define. I chose to examine six separate resources, each of which were initially considered to contribute to the persuasive process.

Three are items the president may use when bargaining with others: favors, flexibility, and rapport. Political favors can be razor-sharp tools of persuasion. Be it in the form of presidential seats at the Kennedy Center or support for a strategically placed public works project in the appropriate congressional district, the president is at liberty to share the perks of his office with Congress in what can be an effective way to amass support. Lest it be assumed that such actions are characteristic of all presidential initiatives, consider the oft-mentioned reluctance of President Carter to engage in horse-trading during his failed energy campaign. If differences in persuasive ability are posited as an explanation for why Carter failed whereas Reagan realized his budget objectives, this may be partly understood by differences in the way the two men used favors. President Carter's determined effort to distance himself from the muck of politics may be contrasted with President Reagan's inclination to conduct shop, in the words of one congressional Democrat, "like a tobacco auction."[28]

Of course, if the sheer number of favors offered translated into effective persuasion, then power would be rather easy to exercise. Finding the appropriate favor, offering it at the right time, and doing so in a way that will endear rather than offend the recipient are all part of the art of persuasion. These actions may be captured in the extent to which the president is effective with his use of favors, in the response he gets when the resource is used. Thus, Ronald Reagan fared well as auctioneer during his successful policy pursuits, as witnessed by the comments of recipients.[29] As we will see, he was not alone.

Along with offering favors, having a flexible nature may contribute to the persuasive process. Engaging in compromise, giving ground, and making concessions are all forms of personal flexibility that may be useful to the president. Jimmy Carter was commonly viewed during his energy drive as rigid and dogmatic, in sharp contrast to the widespread perception of a flexible—and triumphant—Reagan in 1981. Of course, popular views are often wrong. In fact, it will become apparent that both Carter and Reagan, like all presidents, exhibited both flexibility and great stubbornness at various points in their presidencies, with interesting implications for the policy matters on their respective agendas at the time.

Closely related to flexibility is rapport, or an atmosphere of good will between individuals. By virtue of his position, any presidential olive branch is likely to be taken seriously; and if he so desires, the president may work to establish good feelings with members of Congress and the Washington community. Because of this, rapport may be seen as a "resource" for facilitating the persuasive process, even though it is abstract in nature and not normally regarded as something to be "used." A good politician who appreciates the value of the working environment may "use" good feelings to instill a sense of indebtedness in others. In turn, it is just as possible not to develop such feelings, or even purposely to leave the object of persuasion with a bad taste in his mouth. Like flexibility, the desire to encourage good will varies with circumstances, reflecting the president's inclination to bargain while contributing to his persuasive possibilities.

Favors, personal flexibility, and rapport as elements of persuasion are geared to win the affections of potential adversaries, those with no opinion, or anyone who might stand in the president's way. When I speculate that the Carter energy initiative may have failed partly for want of their effective use, I am really suggesting that Carter lacked the persuasive skills associated with bargaining. Borrowing terminology derived by Light,[30] I distinguish bargaining from domination. In the latter sense, a president may persuade by overpowering others rather than by trying to ingratiate them to him. The two forms of persuasion are not mutually exclusive; indeed, Lyndon Johnson was notorious for "the treatment," which blended ego-massage and arm twisting.[31] However, they are conceptually distinct, so the resources constituting the darker side of persuasion—pressure, threats, and sanctions—will be discussed separately.

If Ronald Reagan effectively dominated select congressmen en route to his budget triumph, one way this might be captured is in his reputed ability to engage in pressure tactics. With Reagan, known for the soft sell, the hammer had a velvet cover, but pressure is pressure, be it from Ronald Reagan's gentle reminder of one's obligation to party and government or Lyndon Johnson's icy stare. Folklore and literature alike are replete with instances of presidents turning on the pressure in an effort to squeeze — or bludgeon — opposing forces into line. What we will discover shortly is the facility of pressure campaigns rests more with the heat generated by favors than with the fire of a threat or sanction.

This is because threats and sanctions themselves prove to be less than efficacious resources in the power game. As employed here, threats are verbal promises of ill will that may be acted upon by the president if he so desires. Sanctions are the pursuant actions. Therefore, if the president promises to veto a bill, he is making a threat; if he actually does it, he is imposing a sanction. Of course, threats may take numerous forms, may be issued on a one-to-one basis or to Congress as a whole, and may be baldly evident or subtle and masked. In any form, the president draws on a resource in his arsenal, presumably because he believes it will contribute to his long-range objectives. More often than not, he is misguided in this belief.

The reader will probably note a certain artificial distinction among some of these resources. Although it may be possible to separate bargaining from domination, one may stretch only so far before smudging the line between a favor and the pressure that it may generate, or between presidential flexibility and the rapport it may create. There will be overlap because, as noted earlier, it is hard to identify the specifics of persuasion, but this is done in the effort to identify when and how it works. Subsequently, when exploring the way resources interact with one another, I will attempt more precise statements about the interrelationship among persuasion's component parts.

The other elements of power do not pose the same complications. Neither are they all as personality centered as the resources of persuasion. When we assert that Reagan's ability to establish interpersonal rapport enhanced his budget case or that Carter's personal disdain for backscratching damaged his energy chances, it is of course implied that effective persuasion is a function of the persuader, of his interpersonal skills, his orientation toward others, his behavior. But, if we consider that coordination within the White House may also have been a contributing factor, the argument shifts to a completely different domain.

Published reports indicate the Reagan White House was better equipped to deal effectively with Congress during the budget drive than the Carter White House was during the energy initiative. Where Reagan's lieutenants were widely perceived to be so well prepared as to "know what brand of cigars Speaker O'Neill smokes,"[32] Carter's people were tagged with a reputation for "poor preparation and follow-through."[33] These conditions were not lost on congressional representatives, and the results each president attained were influenced in part by the degree of internal coordination among pertinent top advisors, within the congressional liaison team, and among whatever executive units were mobilized for each effort. This holds repeatedly for other presidential initiatives across administrations: enough so that it can be inferred that efficiency in the executive branch is akin to successful outcomes, a component of presidential power.

This is an especially important avenue to pursue, because traditionally presidential power has not been viewed from an organizational standpoint. We may not think of internal coordination as a useful resource for bringing people around to our perspective, because the others directly involved in the effort are allies in the fight who presumably do not need to be convinced of the merits of the undertaking. Only when we consider the possibility that preparation enhances follow-through does it become reasonable to suggest that coordination and organization may be part of the overall effort. Activity behind the scenes will therefore be examined for its relationship to successful outcomes, and presidential power will be addressed as a mixture of resources, both personal and organizational.

Organizational efficiency, as it is used here, is a power resource and not a product of circumstance, because it is something over which the president has control. Even though the sheer size of the operation may make finding and putting out fires difficult, it is still within the president's province to make the effort. He has the ultimate say as to whether his surrogates stay or go, and it is plainly within his jurisdiction to take action in the event that unwanted internal cleavages form. Such action may be sweeping and salient, as when Jimmy Carter returned from Camp David midway through his term to clean house at the highest levels. More likely, it will be subtle and less well publicized. Without a doubt, internal White House politics will come into play. But, this is exactly what is to be expected from a resource with bearing on presidential power.

The nature of access between the president or his surrogates and members of the Washington community is presented as an additional explanation for why the Carter and Reagan cases ended differently, and this will be offered as another element of presidential power. Access is the second cousin to organizational efficiency; if the latter is in force when members of the executive branch are speaking the same language, the former occurs when they are speaking to Congress.

Open lines of communication between the branches do not occur automatically. Consider the analogous roles played by David Stockman and James Schlesinger in their respective initiatives. Each was entrusted by the president with a large share of the responsibility for their programs, especially in the critical early stages of development. But, where Stockman communicated with others outside OMB, Schlesinger was widely perceived by Congress, and for that matter by many in the White House, to work in secrecy. Not only did this lack of internal communication exacerbate Carter's problems of internal coordination, but it typified the administration's limited interactions with those outside the White House as well.

It should be evident why access is hypothesized to play a role in the scheme of power. If power is partly a product of persuasion, personal contact should be a prerequisite for both effective bargaining and domination. Perhaps some of the threats can be issued at a distance or through the media, perhaps gestures of flexibility can be sent through the grapevine, but by and large the most direct source of contact would be expected to derive from first-person interactions between the president and those he seeks to persuade. In the same vein, when organizational efficiency contributes to presidential power, it is not because of anything the White House does in isolation, but because of the effect the White House has on the policy community. The impact would be felt through channels of access, most notably between the White House and Congress.

The final three factors considered, for which little empirical support was found, derive from noted individual characteristics of Reagan and Carter. From Reagan, I contemplated the possibility that successful policy initiatives are characterized by the effective use of charm and charisma. Given President Reagan's reputation for personal charm, which to some journalists was the driving force behind many of his accomplishments, it seemed reasonable to investigate the possibility that being charming makes a regular contribution to policy success. Of course, for this to have been the case, not only would Reagan need to have come across as charming during the course of his budget battle and Carter as anything but charismatic in the days of the energy case, but both men would have to have reversed roles, so to speak, during other initiatives when the outcomes were different.

From Carter, who was widely noted for his technical proficiency and long working days, two other possible power resources were considered: technical competence or expertise, in the form of facility with information and detail; and initiative, in the form of time and energy invested in an undertaking. Two of President Carter's hallmarks were his grasp of detail and the long hours he spent at the Oval Office. However, if they were factors in a failure of the magnitude of the energy program, one might wonder about their utility to success in general. But hearsay and conventional wisdom can be misleading, making the role of expertise and initiative worth exploring. Indeed, *both* Carter and Reagan appeared to work hard on their respective first-year initiatives.

In each instance, we need to know how presidential resources were perceived by other players in the power game before any firm conclusions may be drawn. More important, we need to know about the general relationship between resources and success before any statements may be made about the overall role of presidential resources in the exercise of power. This requires examining the data. It is to such an examination that we now turn, beginning with the resources of persuasion that facilitate bargaining.

THREE

Bargaining as Persuasion

In Hollywood, if not in Washington, the effective politician demonstrates a smooth and easy personal style that often incorporates extroversion with largess. Outgoing, flexible, and willing to deal, the consummate politician is one who can make others feel at ease and satisfied while their vote or endorsement is being won. If this characterization is exaggerated in the movies, it nonetheless has currency with some who have observed or participated in the Washington power structure. Indeed, when Jimmy Carter is criticized for lacking political instincts, it is for the want of these very characteristics. Consider the observations of Hugh Sidey, made during Carter's first frustrating year:

> Splashing a little bourbon over the ice with Senators like Russell Long or spending an evening cruising down the Potomac with House Speaker Tip O'Neill, listening to his Boston stories, or winking at a few pet water projects may not be what Carter had in mind when he came to the capital. But right or wrong, the ways of government have grown up over two centuries. They are not apt to be discarded or reformed by anyone who stands disapprovingly at arm's length.[1]

Sidey is simply personifying Neustadt's assertion that "the power to persuade is the power to bargain." In an institutional setting that demands compromise precede progress, the president virtually is forced to sway:

> With the array of vantage points at his disposal, a President may be far more persuasive than his logic or his charm could make him. But outcomes are not guaranteed by his advantages. There remain the counter pressures those whom he would influence can bring to bear on him from vantage points at their disposal. Command has limited utility; persuasion becomes a give and take.[2]

The findings I will present in the next few pages support this. During thirty-four policy cases spanning five administrations, chief executives from Johnson to Reagan were consistently engaged in efforts to persuade those in Congress and the executive branch who were needed to promote the president's agenda. Persuasion may take the form of bargaining, as Neustadt suggests, if the president engages in give and take with others in the policy community. This could involve the use of tools designed to get others to move, such as presidential favors, flexibility in negotiation, and the development of an atmosphere of rapport between the president and others. Persuasion may also be exercised through dominance, through presidential efforts to strong-arm, threaten or sanction those who will not support him.

At any point, a president may choose to employ one or several of these resources of persuasion as part of the exercise of power, in an effort to garner political support for something he wants. Likewise, those engaged in the exercise with him will from time to time comment upon what the president did and did not do, making public the details of how the president behaved, of whether persuasive actions were called into play. As a simple measure of the degree to which recent presidents have engaged in the persuasive process during domestic policy crusades, consider the percentage of references by policy actors to the use of these six resources that constitute persuasion: favors, flexibility, rapport, pressure, threats, and sanctions. The relevant data may be found in Table 3.1.

In the aggregate, the five presidents from Johnson to Reagan tended to rely on these resources more often than they overlooked them. But reliance was most heavy during the cases among the

Table 3.1. Mentions of Presidential Persuasion

	Carter		Reagan		34 Cases	
Total Mentions* of	Success	Failure	Success	Failure	Success	Failure
Presidential Persuasion Used (%)	86	54	87	53	88	56
Presidential Persuasion Not Used (%)	14	46	13	47	12	44
Number	(206)	(226)	(348)	(277)	(648)	(577)

*Percent of mentions on the general topic. In the first instance, 86 percent of those commenting on presidential persuasion perceived it to be used.

thirty-four examined that are characterized as successes, when the president realized the domestic policy objective at issue. Table 3.1 allows for comparisons across all cases, as well as for specific comparisons between the eight Carter and Reagan cases, which will be used for illustrative purposes throughout this book.

For all cases—successes and failures—policy actors in a position to be an object of presidential persuasion perceived each of the five chief executives to engage in efforts at opinion swaying or arm twisting more often than not. Even at times when these presidents did not succeed, 56 percent of 577 references included some mention of their attempt to persuade. In general, presidents seem quite aware of "the ways of government" of which Sidey speaks, and the benefits to be derived from using them to their advantage.

Even more striking is the fact that persuasion is present during policy successes at a rate that is 32 percentage points greater than that evident during policy failures. During the successful ventures, 88 percent of 648 references to the resources of persuasion contained mention of their use.

Contemporary presidents are largely aware of the give and take demanded by political circumstance. More important, there is a relationship between their actions and the results they get. But, we will see that this relationship holds almost exclusively for those resources of persuasion designed to encourage bargaining. Efforts to bargain were particularly intense and effective in advance of instances when these presidents successfully achieved their objectives, signaling an important role for the frequent and skillful use of resources of bargaining in the pursuit of presidential power, while suggesting that motivating and not dominating others lies at the heart of the persuasive process.

Presidential attempts at persuasion through domination do not bear much relationship to the results the president attains, as we will see in Chapter 4. Attempts to threaten other Washington actors, or to impose presidential sanctions do not strengthen the president's power position the way bargaining may. Persuasion is best accomplished when the president endears himself to others, rather than when he attempts to persuade by punishing; over the course of the past five administrations, the presidential agenda has been advanced more with the carrot than with the stick. We will see that people respond to presidential bargaining; if practiced skillfully, it is a useful tool, unmatched in its effectiveness by attempts to persuade through domination. But deployment is far from automatic, and its utility is bounded by the extent to which the president understands and controls particular resources that contribute to the bargaining process.

I will address three such resources: personal flexibility, favors, and rapport. Individually the three are quite different. Collectively, they encompass necessary if not sufficient elements of bargaining as persuasion. Flexibility addresses the president's willingness or ability to bend with changing events, to compromise and alter course in an attempt to find common ground with other policy actors who, as Neustadt suggests, have their own agendas and interests. Favors are more tangible, constituting the wide variety of perks available to the president by virtue of his position, which by their very nature are of value to others in the president's purview. They range from small personal mementos bearing the presidential seal, to gifts of status, such as invitations to White House functions, to tacit or active presidential support for projects of value to particular states or congressional districts, any of which may be tendered or withheld by the president during the course of bargaining. Rapport is less tangible. It refers to an atmosphere created between the president and others, by actions or words or both, in which effective bargaining may proceed.

Any of these resources may be employed during the course of persuasion. Inasmuch as all parties to a compromise may or may not exhibit flexibility or try to generate rapport, they are not exclusively the province of the president, although given his vantage point in the system, we would expect presidential efforts at bargaining to attract attention, and the absence of presidential initiatives at the same time to generate some notice and comment. Either way, I will focus exclusively on presidential behavior in the effort to illuminate the role played by the use of his resources in the bargaining process.

In some instances, it is easy to understand how a bargaining resource may be perceived to be "used" or "not used"; in others it is not. Thus, it is fairly easy to distinguish perceptions of presidential flexibility from inflexibility by examining references by other parties in the bargaining process to whether or not the chief executive engaged in compromising, giving ground, making concessions, changing direction, and the like. Offers of favors are likewise easy to note and often recorded, but the inverse occurrence—the *failure* to offer favors—is a bit harder to observe systematically. Surprisingly, scattered across the thirty-four cases are a fair number of references, mostly by members of congress, to instances in which they had expected or wished the president to offer something tangible in exchange for support, but in which such offers were not forthcoming. These references will serve as our approximation of instances in which the president did not offer favors, to be contrasted with those occasions in which he did. Rapport, the most ephemeral of the three resources, is the most difficult to pin down. So many things may contribute to rapport, which I see as being the creation of an agreeable atmosphere among individuals in an interpersonal situation, even if for a brief moment, such as the duration of a meeting. References to the president making friends or allies, making others comfortable, or specifically omitting criticism of others are construed to constitute efforts to generate rapport.[3] In contrast, combative or hostile remarks by the president or observations of a tense or angry tone serve as indications that the president was not of a mind to use rapport to facilitate bargaining.

We will consider each of the three resources of bargaining in turn.

Table 3.2. Mentions of Presidential Bargaining, Carter and Reagan

	Carter		Reagan	
Total Mentions of	Success	Failure	Success	Failure
Presidential Flexibility (%)	82	55	62	39
Presidential Inflexibility (%)	18	45	38	61
Number	(45)	(69)	(61)	(166)
President Generates Rapport (%)	100	60	68	32
President Does Not Generate Rapport (%)	0	40	32	68
Number	(5)	(20)	(34)	(34)
President Offers Favors (%)	70	16	96	0
President Does Not Offer Favors (%)	30	84	4	0
Number	(46)	(50)	(56)	(0)

FLEXIBILITY

There may be no bargaining without compromise. At the heart of presidential bargaining power lies the ability to be flexible, to give and take in the effort to win support for an acceptable version of one's plans. During the Carter and Reagan administrations, both presidents were perceived to be relatively more flexible during successful policy endeavors than during unsuccessful ones. As Table 3.2 indicates, better than eight of ten references to the subject during Carter's successful policy efforts incorporate some mention of the president's ability to compromise (N = 45). In failure, Carter was perceived to be more rigid, as only fifty-five percent of sixty-nine references indicated the presence of presidential flexibility. For Reagan, the distinction between being flexible in success and rigid in failure is even sharper. Almost two-thirds of the 166 mentions of this resource derived from Reagan's policy failures note the president's inflexibility—exactly opposite the ratio one finds when the president succeeds. Clearly, perceptions of presidential flexibility are characteristic of presidential success.

Unfortunately, flexibility is not so simple to identify. Consider the widely held views of these two men. Jimmy Carter is often remembered as a stubborn and inflexible individual who often hurt his own cause by failing to consider the political needs of others, yet who nonetheless was too soft to make and stand by tough decisions. Ronald Reagan, in turn, won a popular reputation as a likeable salesman, whose reluctance to bend on budget and tax issues could be written off to the admirable tendency to stand by long-held beliefs. It could be argued that the two presidents exhibited similar characteristics that were interpreted with a different spin; Reagan's insistence on budgetary changes was no more or less heartfelt than Carter's desire to eliminate what he saw as unnecessary water resource projects. Politically, each desire threatened well-established constituencies, making the different reactions to their positions in no way predictable. But, over time, Carter came to be seen as rigid in his position, whereas Reagan's inflexibility developed a more admirable label, that of dogged determination. In part, these generalizations are the result of *post hoc* theorizing about the two administrations, based largely on the memory of events, influenced by their outcomes. As we will see, *at the time* both presidents received a fair amount of negative feedback about their apparent lack of flexibility. The traits themselves need to be considered as they were at the time to be evaluated correctly.

But herein lies the peculiar nature of flexibility: the same behavior may be seen as alternately favorable or unfavorable. Efforts at compromise may be interpreted as a willingness to work with others by a leader serious about achieving consensus or as the undirected doings of a weak, wishy-washy president. Inflexibility may be read as the courageous dedication of a stalwart chief executive, or the stubborn blindness of an overly dogmatic man. The interpretation is left to the beholder. Thus, the way the behavior is received is a more useful indicator of bargaining effectiveness than the behavior itself.

In a sense, this makes things more complex for the president who wishes to enhance his bargaining ability through increased flexibility. The ability to do so involves being able to interpret correctly the way one's actions are received by one's bargaining partners. Although flexibility is associated with success, it is always possible that too much compromise will be interpreted as a weakness, that a perpetual willingness to give and take will be construed as a lack of backbone. More than the behavior itself, the key to the effective use of flexibility rests with the president's ability to read how his actions are perceived.

Furthermore, flexibility should not be seen as a fixed trait, a quality to which the president is or is not inclined. Both Carter and Reagan had moments of flexibility, when they were able to compromise with others in an effort to achieve their goals. Both experienced the opposite, when they absolutely refused to give in or change their position. Sometimes, they exhibited both behaviors during the course of the same policy event. To suggest that the ability to compromise is an element of the individual, that the president either has it or does not, is to misstate the case. Although we often tend to think of people as being stubborn or not, in fact many of us have the capability to be quite flexible at one moment, quite the opposite one moment later.

During his term, Ronald Reagan exhibited what was interpreted to be both willingness to bargain and mammoth inflexibility. The former was evident during the spring of 1981, in which a president who at first developed a "rigid 'no compromise' policy"[4] regarding his budget proposal soon established a more flexible posture.[5] The same president steadfastly refused any compromise on his effort to hold the line on taxes a year later. "When the President is willing to compromise, we'll talk,"[6] declared House Speaker Tip O'Neill in March 1982. But the willingness was long in coming, and ultimately short-lived. For the most part, Reagan held his ground despite the efforts of his advisors to convince him that his inflexibility was hurting him. Typical was the effort by Commerce Secretary Malcolm Baldrige, who said "I broke my pick"[7] in an unsuccessful effort to get Reagan to budge on the tax issue. Reagan's inflexibility even reached the White House Chief of Staff, who was described by colleagues as becoming "increasingly despondent" that spring, as "the president insist[ed] on sticking to principle"[8] on the tax issue. Noted one observer of Reagan, "From the beginning, this was no game and he was not bluffing. He never intended to budge meaningfully from his firm beliefs about ... cutting taxes."[9]

Jimmy Carter could be equally stubborn. On the issue of the water resource projects that the president viewed as an unnecessary pork barrel, Carter refused to budge regardless of the political fallout. " 'He is adamant,' reported key White House lieutenant Hamilton Jordan. 'Like human rights, it's not negotiable.' "[10] Others in the White House underscored this position: "Vice President Mondale ... [said] that far from being prepared to bargain, Carter was determined to see that the projects were ended, because of their costs or questionable benefits or environmental impact."[11] By May 1977, "the failure of President Carter to compromise in his bitter struggle with Congress over those eighteen unwanted water projects reached a humiliating peak when not one of the thirty-seven Democrats on the House Appropriations Committee spoke in his defense ... when the committee approved seventeen of the projects."[12]

The president began work on his energy program with much the same attitude. But, by April 1977, "under prodding, Carter [had] begun to compromise."[13] Although some felt Carter's new-found flexibility came at "the eleventh hour,"[14] and although he was still likely to draw the line in some instances, such as what Senator Russell Long perceived to be a "rigid stand on price controls,"[15] nonetheless Carter was able to deal with Congress. By

August, President Carter had "established a more workable give-and-take relationship with Congress as its members head[ed] home for the summer recess."[16] It was the result of the president's recent willingness "to accept compromises"[17] on important domestic issues like the energy program. At different times, under diverse conditions, these quite different presidents demonstrated both great stubbornness and the inclination to negotiate. Flexibility is a function of circumstance as well as character.

This last point is quite noteworthy: neither president was perceived to be flexible all the time. Even during policy success, when the *ratio* of references to flexibility relative to inflexibility was quite high, both presidents had moments when they were still perceived to be rigid and unbending. During his successful Panama Canal Treaty ratification drive, Jimmy Carter shed his image as "the aloof and didactic technocrat"[18]—albeit late in the campaign—to compromise with senators on treaty specifics, as when the president modified his position on keeping U.S. troops in Panama in order to win the support of Arizona Senator Dennis DeConcini.[19] President Reagan's sudden "burst into the open" with a series of what one observer called "startling accommodations" during his effort to hold the line on taxes came only after key advisors convinced the president that "he appeared to be foundering publicly in his own partisanship and obstinacy."[20] In a more subtle maneuver, Reagan "ordered his staff to repudiate the report that the Administration was willing to compromise on the tax cut portion of his [1981] economic proposals,"[21] despite the climate of compromise the president had fostered in the spring of 1981.

By and large, both Carter and Reagan managed to find a way to make flexibility work for them during their successful policy crusades. The similarity may be found in Panel a of Figure 3.1, which presents data on a rough measure of bargaining effectiveness garnered from the evaluations that occasionally accompanied observations by policy actors of presidential flexibility. When a policy actor made a reference to presidential flexibility that included an evaluative component, it was interpreted and coded on a simple 5-point evaluation scale.[22] Although approximate, the measure distinguishes favorable from unfavorable evaluations to get a better feel for how the aggregate policy community reacted to the president. The scale considers only evaluations by policy ac-

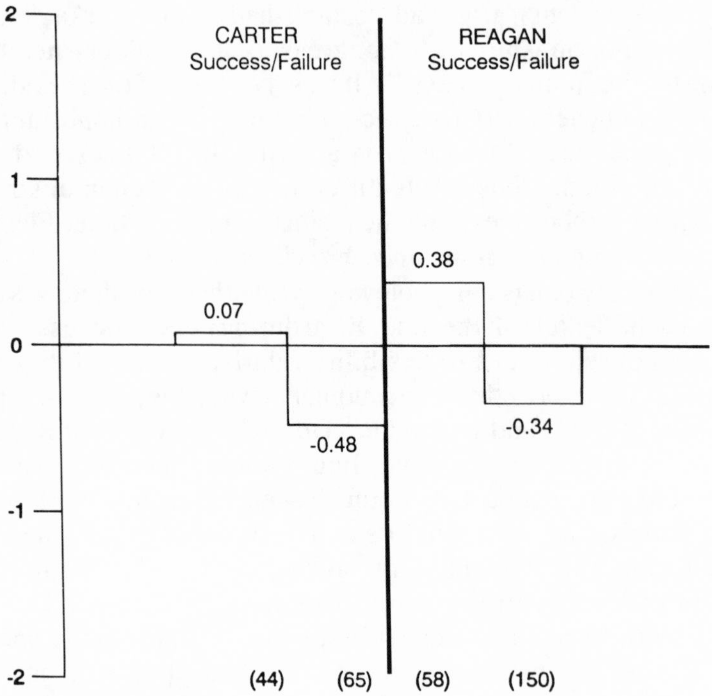

Figure 3.1a. Flexibility

tors that clearly included an assessment of presidential flexibility. For this reason, the number of observations in the figure is less than the total number of observations of presidential flexibility present in Table 3.1.

Although only an approximate measure of effectiveness, it is striking to note how aggregate evaluations of both Carter and Reagan were positive during those instances in which they would ultimately achieve their objectives. Carter was perceived to be slightly effective, on the whole, with the flexibility he demonstrated during his successful endeavors, averaging a rating of +0.07, just slightly above the neutral midpoint of the scale. Reagan was judged more effective, earning a rating of +0.38. Thus, policy success is characterized by both greater flexibility and the tendency for it to be interpreted in a positive light; that is, as a factor that encourages bargaining.

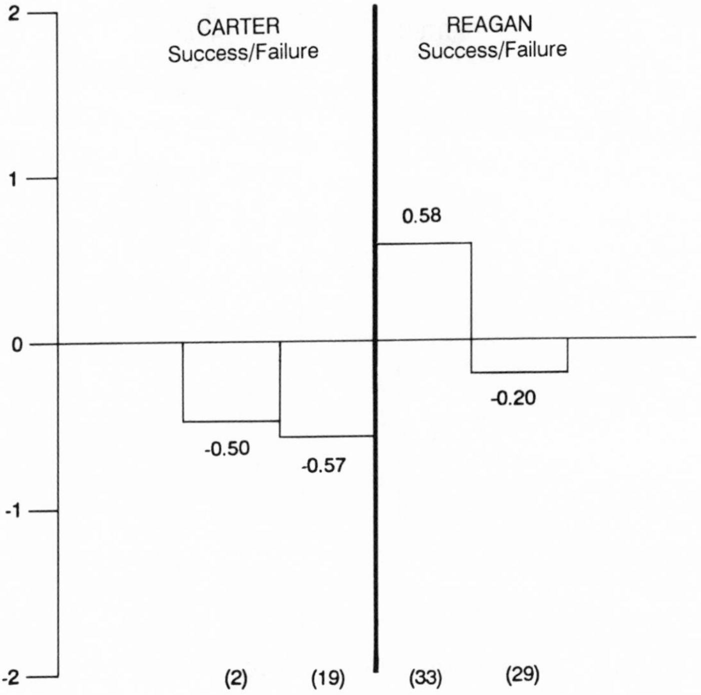

Figure 3.1b. Rapport

Just as Carter and Reagan are perceived to be less flexible during the policy pursuits they would lose, so was their rigidity seen to be a hindrance to their bargaining ability. On average, both presidents ranked poorly on the effectiveness scale, rating comparable scores of −0.48 (Carter) and −0.34 (Reagan). By digging in their heels, they damaged their chances to find common ground with those who were in a position to block their objectives, particularly members of Congress. Most interesting is the comparable nature of the response, both in direction and degree, to the stubbornness of these two chief executives. Despite their different personalities and characters, the Democrat from Georgia and the Republican from California received comparable evaluations (and comparable results) from the policy community for their mutual tendencies to be less flexible during their unsuccessful policy efforts.

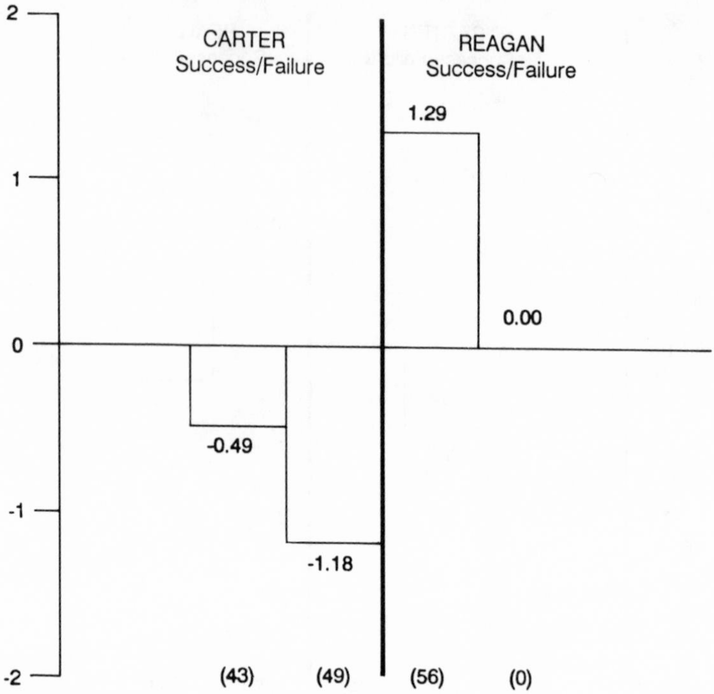

Figure 3.1c. Favors

Figure 3.1. Bargaining Effectiveness, Carter and Reagan

We find, then, several things. Presidents will vary in the degree to which they employ compromise and flexibility in their interpersonal negotiations. Greater flexibility tends to be appreciated, and likely contributes to bargaining effectiveness. Furthermore, presidents appear to employ a flexible approach more often during instances when their efforts bear fruit—a reasonable observation given that flexibility tends to be received well.

However, it is too simple to assert that the president who wishes to maximize his bargaining power should always be flexible. For one thing, it is unrealistic to believe that a person who truly believes taxes or water projects are "nonnegotiable" could simply change his mind for the sake of political expedience. Second, we must not overlook the importance that occasional inflexibility plays in maintaining the value of the resource. If the president is rigid at times, it underscores the importance of the events for which he is willing to compromise, and thus increases the value of flexibility. And, the president who is always willing to accommodate risks being seen as weak.

For the president wishing to employ flexibility to enhance bargaining, timing is critical. To be effective, flexibility needs to be used selectively and communicated carefully, lest the president may be seen at a disadvantage. But, to resist compromise may be even more counterproductive in the long run. The proper mix appears to include more compromise than stubbornness, but no recipe exists to suggest precise measurements. Only the president can sense how his actions are being interpreted and what he may be able to do to further his agenda; at that point, power becomes an art.

RAPPORT

Unlike flexibility, rapport is more an atmospheric quality than a behavior, even if it is generated by things people do. This makes it and its source harder to identify. It is best discussed in general terms, less well defined than some of the other items addressed here. Not surprisingly, the total number of clear references to this resource is quite small. But, as a condition that exists among individuals which has the potential to facilitate bargaining, it is worth considering, albeit briefly.

An example of rapport may help to clarify its meaning. During his successful budget drive, President Reagan not only realized the value of flexibility, but endeavored to create an atmosphere, especially in his dealings with Congress, that would encourage bargaining. To enhance his persuasive position, especially with others who had been in the Capitol much longer than he, the president engaged in what one observer called an "amiable, but persistent courtship of the House."[23] Through his attitude and his approach, Reagan attempted to develop a sense of rapport with Congress that would enable him to work with—to bargain with—the legislature as an equal player. By being amiable, he appealed to endear himself to Congress, rather than anger or alienate those with whom he bargained.

Both Reagan achievements, as well as the two Carter success stories, are characterized by a preponderance of references to this type of amiability, inasmuch as rapport is mentioned as a factor at all. The number of references is small, but during their policy successes both presidents were perceived to operate on the friendly basis discussed earlier, according to the figures in Table 3.2. And, as with flexibility, we again see a different pattern emerge for policy failures, in which the percentage of references to this type of activity is much smaller in relation to instances in which the president was critical, difficult, or inclined to keep others at a distance rather than draw them closer.

Keep in mind that these are relative figures; although rapport was most evident during success, there were apparently some instances in which the president was far from interested in amiability. What appears to be distinguishable between success and failure is the frequency with which rapport was attempted. For instance, while President Reagan was courting Congress, he was also fond of making public statements that tended to mock official Washington, creating distance in the eyes of the public between himself and some of what Reagan often characterized as the crazies who inhabit the shores of the Potomac. It is quite possible that such public statements could exist side-by-side with a gentler interpersonal approach, considering that the targets of the two messages — the public and official Washington — play different roles. But, during his failed policy initiatives, it in fact appeared as if something resembling the public Reagan was doing the bargaining. Two-thirds of the references to rapport in these cases suggest the president failed to assume an amiable stance. In contrast, during Reagan's successes, the ratio of rapport-generating to rapport-frustrating observations is reversed.[24]

Accordingly, if the president is perceived to be collegial, it would follow that he is likely to be evaluated positively on this score. Loosely speaking, the "effective" implementation of rapport rests with the acknowledgment by the president's bargaining partners that the atmosphere is conducive to progress because of the president's gestures. Certainly, as Panel b of Figure 3.1 attests, this was the case during successful Reagan policy cases, where the president merits a mean effectiveness score of +0.58 for his efforts at amiability.[25] The tendency exhibited by both presidents during their failures to be less amiable toward others in the policy community, likewise, was met with far less enthusiastic evaluations. Thus, when Senate Majority Leader Robert Byrd termed Carter's June 1977 criticism of Congress a *mistake*[26] he was reacting to the president's failure to establish an atmosphere of rapport; and as one would expect, he was reacting negatively.

We might consider rapport and flexibility first cousins. The receptivity underlying a willingness to compromise is itself interpretable as a form of rapport, as an openness to considering the wishes of others. When Reagan attempted successfully to endear himself to Congress and the Washington community, the flexibility he demonstrated underscored an apparent willingness to listen, which together enhanced his bargaining position. When the president was more rigid he was also more closed and more likely to be perceived as distant. The same may be said of President Carter, whose flexibility during successful policy endeavors goes hand-in-hand with a sense of rapport that, though sketchy, was less evident during failure, when presidential stubbornness and harsher feelings were more commonplace.

FAVORS

Favors constitute the final piece of the bargaining puzzle. Included here is patronage, or political gifts, and personal favors of all sizes, from the privilege of sitting in the president's box at the Kennedy Center, to state dinner invitations, to the tie clips dispensed freely by President Reagan during his 1981 budget campaign. Usually but not exclusively directed at Congress for the purpose of swaying votes, favors are sometimes considered "the lubricant"[27] of politics, the grease that smoothes the way for people to work together.

The importance of favors to bargaining is obvious—so much so that one would expect to find little variability in their use from president to president or from case to case. Indeed, exchanging favors is the essence of the give-and-take that is bargaining, and the president—every president—has at his easy disposal a host of patronage and prestige-related properties. What makes the data in Table 3.2 so remarkable is the great variation between success and failure in the way Carter and Reagan each employed favors.

At any given time, a policy actor may make reference to the fact that the president offered a favor. Likewise, he or she may comment that a favor would have been appreciated but was not offered or that the president was opposed to a patronage project. The ratio of the former type of comment to the latter serves as an approximate measure of the use of favors as a presidential bargaining resource. During their policy successes, both presidents were perceived to rely on favors rather consistently. For Carter, 70 percent of forty-six references to favors were mentions of times when the president employed them; for Reagan, the comparable figure is an overwhelming 96 percent (N = 56). This translates into a picture of two presidents relying steadily on the perks of their office to sway other Washington actors during those instances in which they were destined to succeed.

In sharp contrast, Ronald Reagan simply did not use favors during his policy failures, whereas Jimmy Carter demonstrated outright hostility to pork-barrel privilege during his. The absence of all references to favors during Reagan policy failures indicates an entirely different kind of activity than that evident during his successful endeavors. During the 1981 budget and 1982 tax cases, the president dispensed favors with abandon, openly attempting to gain leverage over wavering members of Congress. But, during his aborted campaigns for the MX missile and holding the line on taxes, favors simply were not a factor.

If Reagan was neutral to favors during his failures, Carter was downright malevolent. The president assumed a no-compromise attitude toward the removal of water resource projects that themselves were important congressional patronage operations. His floundering effort to eliminate them was at its core antagonistic to the very type of favor a president could use to his advantage. Rather than attempt to substitute other favors for the removal of the projects, Carter simply held his ground against the concept of patronage in general and the projects in particular. The same approach was evident during his failed energy policy, which occurred at the same early stage of his tenure. Collectively, 84 percent of the references to favors made during these two cases (N = 50) mention Carter's refusal to use them, reflecting the president's antipathy to patronage.

The very fact that Carter called the patronage system into question caused observers to stand up and take notice:

> Jimmy Carter is trying to take the pork out of the pork barrel, and Congress wants to leave it in. The basic fight is as simple as that, but the ramifications are enormous, millions of Americans will be affected, the issues are hotly debatable, and the struggle threatens to become the new President's most serious conflict with Capitol Hill.[28]

> Everybody in Congress knows what really is at issue in the public works bill. It's the long-standing congressional practice of logrolling, of mutual back scratching and accommodation, of putting good, bad and mediocre projects into one big bill, then resolutely fending off those who would tear the bill and the pork barrel apart.[29]

For all his noble intentions, Carter did not fulfill his desire to abandon the pork barrel. On the contrary, he was unable to roll back the money targeted for the water projects to a significant degree. He did manage to anger a Congress of his own party, which, after an eight-year absence from power in the White House, was looking forward to the privileges of power flowing freely once more. A similarly negative attitude toward the use of big-ticket favors infiltrated the president's bargaining on the energy issue as well, depleting his ability to persuade. By seeing the set of resources labeled *patronage* as "evils to be eliminated,"[30] Carter damaged his ability to bargain. No matter how well intentioned, he tried to scrape away some of the grease that lubricates the wheels. One observer felt that "the President's failure to make effective use of patronage had undermined party discipline in Congress."[31] One might add that it undermined his own bargaining position as well.

Carter eventually changed his tune. Despite his moral qualms about favor trading, he managed to engage in a fair amount of dealing during the two policy victories addressed here: deregulation of natural gas and Senate ratification of the Panama Canal treaties. During the latter case, for instance, "the President, who had previously disdained swapping favors for votes, . . . asked [undecided Senators] how he could be helpful."[32] Carter found himself able to "scratch and bargain for votes like any other mortal politician,"[33] even on big-ticket policy items that earlier would have been non-negotiable: "The White House quickly changed its position today on the $2.3-billion emergency farm bill to conform to the wishes of a Senator whose vote it is wooing on the Panama Canal treaties."[34] This was a far cry from the more idealistic position Carter had held during the first year of his administration.

It should be added that his newfound ability to offer favors did not exactly overwhelm Congress. Panel c of Figure 3.1 demonstrates the point. During his policy failures, as one would expect, Carter's hostility to back scratching registered strong negative evaluations of his attitude toward favors, most coming from would-be congressional recipients. Carter's effectiveness score of −1.18 is strongly negative, reflecting the consensual nature of the opinion that the president had damaged his bargaining position through his adamant opposition to favor trading. When he loosened his resistance in the pursuit of policy objectives he would ultimately achieve, his score improved to −0.49, but this can hardly be considered stunning. If anything, the president was perceived to be less ineffective rather than more effective, to be hurting his cause less than he had when his resistance to using favors was total.

In truth, Jimmy Carter was never comfortable with favor trading, and this evaluation confirms the fact that he never did it very well. In fact, some of the same people who condemned Carter for failing to employ favors to his advantage in 1977 found themselves criticizing what they felt was a carnival of bargaining during the Panama Canal treaties ratification fight the next year. It was mused that to win the support of Senator Russell Long, Carter had agreed to "the transfer of the whole Louisiana Territory."[35] Senator Bob Packwood said he was "troubled by the fact that so many rumors are rampant"[36] about deals between the president and undecided senators. The president, he said, should not be "master of ceremonies at 'Let's Make A Deal.' "[37] And so, the president who finally realized that his own dedication to an idealized politics was hurting his bargaining position was greeted with displeasure when he tried to employ favors to pursue his ends. Granted, the reaction was far less negative than what Carter had faced earlier. But you get the sense that Carter was struggling with favors, unable or unsure exactly how to use them smoothly and appropriately. Like his progress in the two cases themselves, success came at last, but only after much effort. If Carter never fully grasped the way to use favors, he nonetheless did better than he had when his personal objection to the politics of the pork barrel helped keep him from advancing his agenda.

Ronald Reagan's approach couldn't have been more different. Unburdened by the ethical dilemmas that racked his predecessor, the Californian was able to deluge a willing Congress with perks during his 1981 budget drive and his 1982 tax hike campaign — without bringing upon himself the torrent of criticism that Carter faced. From the first battle, Reagan made it plain that his message would be, "we'll be around for four years, and we can do a lot of things for you."[38] The sentiment was directed both toward Republicans and wavering members of the opposition. For instance,

> Representative Carroll Hubbard, Jr. [had] represented western Kentucky for seven years, but he [attended] a state dinner at the White House [in May 1981] for the first time in his Washington career. That invitation, to a dinner for the Prime Minister of Japan, [was] just one small part of the extraordinary lobbying campaign focusing on forty-four conservative Democrats from the south and the west who [were important to] the fate of President Reagan's buget proposals in the House of Representatives.[39]

Nor were favors limited to "Sunday lunch at Camp David,"[40] a perk extended to over 150 congressmen whose vote was essential on the tax measure. Reagan felt quite comfortable dwelling in territory where his predecessor initially feared to tread. During both drives, "political favors were dispensed freely. Representative Norman Lent of New York," for instance, "was promised that the A-10 Thunderbolt II attack plane, made on Long Island, would not be phased out as planned if he voted for the tax bill. Lent 'agonized,' then supported the President."[41]

During each campaign, the White House was quite aware of what was happening. One White House aide said of the activity during the tax crusade, " 'this is the biggest shopping spree we've gone through.' "[42] Said another staffer during the budget drive, " 'there's a good argument ... that we gave away the store.' "[43] The president's actions were not lost on those who benefited, either. Unlike Jimmy Carter, who could not seem to perform the master-of-ceremonies role comfortably, Ronald Reagan was perceived to be quite effective with his use of favors during these two successful campaigns, meriting an effectiveness score of +1.29. Reagan was as effective with favors when he succeeded as Carter was ineffective with favors when he failed. The Reagan White House looked no less like "Let's Make A Deal"; Ronald Reagan simply made a better Monty Hall.

Given this, the absence of favors during the two failed Reagan cases stands in surprising contrast to what one might expect from a president so successful with them at other times. During his failed policies, Reagan simply did not attempt the favor trading that characterized the budget and tax episodes. This may partly reflect the important realization that one cannot run the presidency like a game show all the time. The president can offer many favors, but if he does so continuously he risks devaluing them and the advantage they bring him. Far from being able to "buy" a victory, the president needs to be aware of the fact that he should pinpoint his objectives carefully and "spend" where it matters most. Like flexibility, using the resource all the time may lead others to believe that what the president offers is their right to have, not a privilege for which to be grateful.

It is quite possible, too, that the MX case simply did not lend itself to a shopping spree. The president attempted to win approval of the missile with the Dense Pack basing scheme during a "lame duck" session of Congress, which met for a brief time following the election. Political favors that would have been of maximum benefit prior to the election had limited impact at this time, and it is quite likely that the president chose not to play his full bargaining hand because of it. But, in so doing, Reagan pushed the MX project without the benefit of one resource he had manipulated so skillfully during earlier successes, leaving him in a weaker position to bargain.

CONCLUSIONS

Perhaps the most striking thing about bargaining is the extent to which it is related to the outcomes recent presidents have achieved. Carter and Reagan serve as good illustrations. By and large, when they were flexible, amiable, and served up the perks of their office, they subsequently achieved their policy ends. When they were unyielding, disagreeable, and did not employ favors, they realized less fortunate results. If good bargaining rests with generating a favorable environment for others, then a president who knows how to use these tools will be able to increase his persuasive power.

But, this leads to an observation that is equally striking: no president — not even the highly touted Ronald Reagan, whose interpersonal skills are now legendary — uses his bargaining resources to their fullest extent all the time. If the relationship between their use and successful outcomes is so strong, it may appear a bit surprising that anything less than a total effort is made. Yet, we find the Reagan favor machine of 1981 silent during the MX case, as we find the Carter of 1978 who could compromise during the Panama Canal debate to be a seemingly different person than the dogmatic president of a year before.

The reason for these differences, I believe, is partly circumstance, partly necessity. Presidential willingness to bargain will vary with the situation. If President Carter had not come to Washington with disdain for (some would call it ignorance to the importance of) large-scale pork-barrel politics, he may have been more willing to trade favors to smooth the way for the energy program he wanted. If President Reagan had not long loathed the tax increase, he may have been more flexible when those around him pleaded with him to recognize the need for one; certainly, he exhibited great flexibility in other instances. But all circumstances are not alike, and presidents, as human beings, will not react evenly to situations they do not feel warrant comparable behavior, even if it means jeopardizing a policy they want.

On top of this, resources are limited in availability, even to presidents. To throw favors at policy actors every time something important comes along is to devalue the resource and possibly the importance of the individual using it. A carefully placed presidential invitation to a state function can be a memorable—and persuasive — experience. If it's done on a regular basis, however, it can lose its force and even come to be expected. It is one thing for the president to flatter a member of Congress with a personal phone call at home; it is quite another if when the phone rings late at night it's the president *again*.

As politicians, presidents are no doubt aware of this instinctively and realize that choices have to be made. Targets for bargaining need to be chosen carefully, and bargaining needs to be employed when the potential payoff is greatest. It is hard to put a number on the limits of presidential resources, on how much the president can try to bargain during an administration before his resources lose their effectiveness. Part of this rests with how skillfully they are used. Apparently, presidents can flood Washington with favors or demonstrate great flexibility over the course of a single case with quite favorable effect. But, to do so continuously would be a different matter.

☆ ☆ ☆ ☆ ☆ ☆ ☆ ☆

Bargaining performs a central role in the process of persuasion. Three resources of bargaining available to the president—personal flexibility, rapport in interpersonal dealings, and the use of favors—are all related to the outcome the president attains. Policy successes are characterized by a tendency for the president to appear flexible without seeming uncommitted, in sharp contrast to policy failures, which tend to be associated with greater rigidity by the chief executive. Likewise, presidents tend to generate an atmosphere of rapport more effectively during policy successes, smoothing the way for successful bargaining. Favors, as well, play a key role in the process of bargaining. During their successful endeavors, both Carter and Reagan relied most heavily on favors ranging from small presidential perks to large-scale pork-barrel politics. The failures experienced by both men were markedly different, with Reagan not using favors and Carter demonstrating hostility to playing politics with public works projects. Overall, the president's ability to persuade others to accept his position rests with the effective use of the resources that enhance his bargaining power.

FOUR

Domination as Persuasion

Compromise is persuasive, as is rapport. People often have difficulty turning down favors, especially when gilded with a presidential touch. By bargaining, the president may enhance his chances of effecting the policy outcome he desires. Domination, however, is a different story. Threatening other players may make the president feel better, but it will not move them closer to his ends. Sanctions are of equally limited utility. If the president could hold a knife to the throat of official Washington, this reality could be different; with no way to escape, domination can be quite persuasive. But by constitutional design, the president is not an effective knifewielder. The ability to pressure, threaten, or impose sanctions may be available to him, but he faces Congress and his own executive branch as only one among many, blessed with numerous resources, of course, but not free to use them all without recourse. He may threaten Congress with the wrath of the presidency, but so often the legislature simply ignores the threat or, worse, is offended by it and moves farther away from supporting the president's position. The footing between Congress and the president is even enough to make the chief executive's efforts at domination moot or counterproductive.

The single exception to this is when the president places pressure on others, especially those in Congress. As we will see, this is the case almost all the time, during policy failures as well as accomplishments. But, during failure, pressure is perceived as less effective, indicating a relationship between pressuring Congress and presidential achievement. In this limited sphere, the president may be seen to impose his wishes effectively. But, as domination goes, pressure is hardly one's strongest weapon. It is as much a first cousin to bargaining as a tool of domination, a condition that could be generated as much by offering favors as by making threats. The big guns are threats and sanctions, and these are of limited utility. They may even hurt the president's cause.

The three resources of domination are fairly easy to identify. They form the core of the items the president might use when trying to change minds more through arm twisting than endearment. Pressure accounts for times in which the president was perceived to push home a point, in most instances by members of Congress. Of all the resources of persuasion, pressure is most like rapport: a condition between individuals that the president may create, not a tangible item like a favor or a threat. It may be generated by a host of behaviors, including the three resources discussed in the previous chapter. Pressure is included as a resource of domination because its use is designed to push someone into accepting the president's position, no matter how harsh or gentle its application may be. Offering a favor may—indeed should—generate pressure on the recipient, just as readily as might the harsh words of a presidential threat. I selected to examine the pressure generated by other behaviors separately to understand more fully the source of the responses produced by the president's actions.

Threats and sanctions are quite clearly tools of domination, opposite in intent from favor giving and efforts to compromise. The two are closely related. When the president's words indicate that he intends to punish others by withholding something they want, he makes a threat. When he carries out a threat or simply acts in a manner that denies something that another wants, he imposes a sanction. Sanctions may or may not follow from threats, but they are always supported by actions. Thus, it is a threat when a president says he'll veto a bill if something in the bill is not changed. If the bill is actually vetoed, it is a sanction.

Any of these resources may be observed by policy actors to be used or not used. A member of Congress, for insance, may note that the president applied pressure in the course of a meeting or through an action, or that an opportunity to use pressure was not seized. Threats and sanctions, as well, may be witnessed by policy actors or anticipated but not made. Likewise, the pure number of mentions of these resources may provide additional clues to their utility. Such is the case with sanctions, to which there were practically no references during the thirty-four policy cases examined. If the use of sanctions occurred in private, they would not have been captured by this research effort. Although this is possible, it is hard to imagine the widespread use of something as salient as sanctions to escape the public record over a period of almost two decades. Some sanctions, like the veto, were employed at times, but these were few and far between. Simply put, sanctions are not a major part of the president's arsenal. When the president attempts to dominate, he travels other avenues. We will explore two of these and discover that pressure is a useful byway, though not one that is completely related to domination, whereas threats are simply a dead end.

PRESSURE

Although pressure may be real or anticipated, it is not surprising that most of the references to pressure in Table 4.1 indicate that it was used. Whether attempting to bargain or dominate, pressure is fundamental to any presidential effort at persuasion. During successful and failed policies alike, Presidents Carter and Reagan were perceived to take advantage of the opportunities they had to apply pressure on others, according to the recipients of that pressure. In this respect, the simple application of pressure appears to be unrelated to the outcome the president attains.[1]

It was quite typical to feel, as one Reagan observer put it, "a drumbeat of pressure"[2] from the Reagan and Carter White House. Common to all policy cases were references to "putting on the pressure,"[3] as Jimmy Carter was perceived to do during the Panama Canal treaties ratification effort, or to "turning the screws"[4] on Congress, as President Reagan was perceived to do during his 1981 budget drive. The motivation, to paraphrase then White House Chief of Staff James Baker, was the belief that "constant

Table 4.1. Mentions of Presidential Pressure, Carter and Reagan

	Carter		Reagan	
Total Mentions* of	Success	Failure	Success	Failure
Presidential Pressure Applied (%)	95	68	99	97
Presidential Pressure Not Applied (%)	5	32	1	3
Number	(107)	(57)	(165)	(59)

*Percent of mentions on the general topic. In the first instance, 95 percent of those commenting on presidential pressure perceived that it was applied.

pressure will force congressional opponents to support [the president] as the price of political survival.''[5]

Even during times when these presidents did not succeed, the pressure was on. And, it could take numerous forms. For President Reagan, pressure was often gently but relentlessly applied during the course of interpersonal dealings with Congress, a product of the way the president exploited the access he had to others: ''At his residence, Mr. Reagan continued to lobby for his economic package by telephone. White House officials said that the President would be calling several dozen members of Congress this week, especially House Democrats who might defect from their leadership's policies and support the President's package.''[6] White House aides both ''privately and in public statements'' admitted that the point of the endeavor was ''to pressure Congress through the force of Mr. Reagan's popularity,''[7] although such efforts continued later in the term, when the president's standing with the public was not as great.

Likewise, pressure may be indirectly applied. This was often President Carter's approach. During the Panama Canal treaties campaign, considered by some to be ''one of the most intensive White House lobbying campaigns in many years,''[8] presidential pressure was often felt through third parties, as when Carter ''enlisted the efforts of one of the country's top gospel disk jockeys'': ''Coincidentally or not, the Baptist preacher exerts his greatest influence in the backyard of Senator Howard H. Baker Jr., Republican of Tennessee, the Senate minority leader, whose decision on the canal treaties is regarded by many as crucial to its passage.''[9] In the same vein, the president attempted to create pressure on the Senate by telling a ''town meeting'' of his concern that ''Cuba or other Communist countries might be tempted to try to create dissension in Panama''[10] should the treaties not be ratified.

If pressure may take many forms and even have multiple sources, so may its repercussions vary. It is with the impact of pressure that we find the one indication that its use contributes to the outcomes a president achieves. Although we cannot attribute variation in the use of pressure to policy outcomes, given the uniform reliance by Carter and Reagan on pressure during all their policy cases, there is a relationship between the aggregate reactions of those experiencing presidential pressure and the results each president achieved. During their policy successes, Carter and Reagan were deemed most effective with the pressure they applied.

References to presidential effectiveness with pressure are derived from mentions of the resource that include an evaluation by the observer. Effectiveness is measured roughly on the same simple 5-point scale used in the previous chapter (see Figure 4.1). Both Carter and Reagan chalk up aggregate positive evaluations of their use of pressure during policy successes, although with an evaluation of +0.70, Reagan is perceived to have been more effective than Carter, who merits a rating of +0.38. Policy actors reacted to pressure in these instances by acknowledging, in word or in deed, the influence it was exerting on them. When Nevada Senator Paul Laxalt exclaimed that Carter's Panama Canal effort " 'was absolutely unbelievable,' "[11] he was referring to the fact that

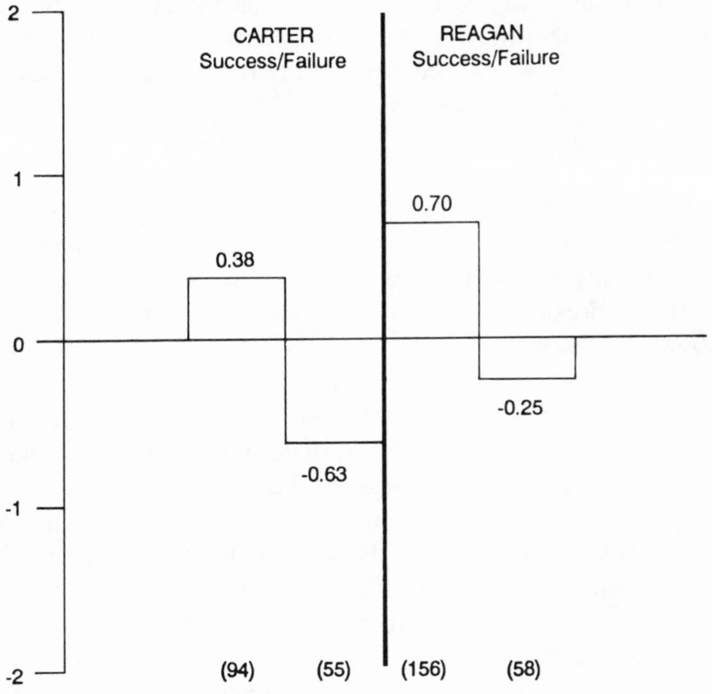

Figure 4.1. Effectiveness with Pressure, Carter and Reagan

the President was successfully applying massive pressure on undecided senators. More concretely, Carter got results from his pressure campaign, albeit at times grudgingly: "Under pressure from the Carter administration, Senator Dennis DeConcini agreed 'reluctantly' . . . to soften a controversial reservation that he was proposing to the second Panama Canal treaty."[12]

Of course, when pressure was not well received, policy actors were more than willing to express this fact as well. This tended to be the case during both Carter and Reagan policy failures, although just as he was more effective with pressure when he succeeded, President Reagan was not evaluated as harshly as his predecessor when he failed. Either way, the differences in evaluations of pressure between success and failure are clear for both Carter and Reagan, who received effectiveness scores of −0.63 and −0.25, respectively, during their unsuccessful policy efforts. Sometimes, members of Congress felt pressure was unduly applied, as when certain senators were "angered" by Panama Canal lobbying.[13] Other times, they simply felt presidential pressure was off the mark, as when Senator Robert Byrd said that President Carter had "failed to lobby effectively"[14] for his energy program. On average, such negative evaluations are associated with presidential policy failures.

The condition that presidents create when they effectively put on the pressure reflects the effective use of other resources as it pinpoints the pressure itself as a motivating force in moving others toward the president's position. As such, pressure itself and the resources from which it may be derived are both useful components in the arsenal of presidential persuasion. But, if the resources that generate pressure are bargaining tools, then it can hardly be said that the president can dominate others through the careful and effective use of pressure. Rather, it is more accurate to say that the effective use of pressure evident during policy successes is testimony to the fact that the president is bargaining well. Effective bargaining *should* build pressure, even as it brings others closer to the president's position. Implicit in the use of favors is the obligation, tacit or spoken, by the recipient to be open to the wishes of the favor giver. Central to taking a flexible position is the enhanced obligation of other bargainers to respond in kind. Both circumstances rely on pressure for their effectiveness. That we find Carter and Reagan to be most effective with pressure during their successes even though pressure is found to be applied extensively in success and failure is further evidence that the resources of bargaining discussed in the previous chapter are taking their toll. Nothing intrinsic to pressure as a resource works to move policy actors; the president cannot apply a thing called *pressure* in an effort to dominate others. He can, however, build pressure through effective bargaining.

If there were a relationship between policy outcomes and the other resources of domination, we might be able to make the same statement about these resources and the pressure they create. But, the initial relationship is not there. In fact, in the case of threats, a resource designed to dominate appears to have exactly the opposite effect.

THREATS

Few references to threats were found among the data on the Carter and Reagan policy cases. However, the pattern that emerges from the several clear mentions of threats coded for the eight cases suggests an interesting, if tentative, conclusion. Table 4.2 divides the mentions of presidential threats into two groups: references that indicate a threat was made; and those that suggest none was forthcoming, even though policy actors felt that circumstances were ripe for one.

Most occurrences are of the first type, when actual threats were made. Even so, the highest proportion of these references occurred during the policy *failures* of the two presidents. Of the twenty-nine mentions of threats occurring during Carter's failed policy efforts, eighty-six percent are references to threats made. The comparable figure for Reagan's failures is eighty-eight percent

Table 4.2. Mentions of Presidential Threats, Carter and Reagan

	Carter		Reagan	
Total Mentions of	Success	Failure	Success	Failure
Presidential Threats Made (%)	67	86	79	88
Threats Anticipated but Not Made (%)	33	14	21	12
Number	(3)	(29)	(28)	(16)

(N = 16). This compares with figures that are slightly lower for both presidents when they succeeded.

Plainly put, presidents can threaten but others—especially those in Congress—don't have to listen. Whereas it may be overstating things to say that the more presidents threaten the less likely they are to attain their ends, the greatest proportion of threats is associated with presidential defeats for a limited number of observations. Carter and Reagan certainly did not advance their agendas by conjuring up images of the blow with a stick.

Moreover, many of the threats that were made were simply disregarded by the intended recipients. For instance, during his unsuccessful attempt to block the water resource projects early in his administration, "President Carter threatened ... to use his veto power if Congress voted what he called 'excessive' increases in spending, but Congress did not appear to be in a mood to heed such warnings."[15] According to this observer, the threat simply worked to increase the "ideological estrangement"[16] between Carter and a Congress of his own party. Around the same time, during Carter's failed energy initiative, a threat that was intended to persuade Congress to advance the proposal simply backfired, as the Senate Finance committee "voted by 10 to 6 to prohibit increases in duties on oil imports except in wartime. The proposal, by Senator Robert Dole, Republican of Kansas, was in response to threats by the Administration that it would use its existing authority to impose a duty of $5 a barrel if its proposed tax on domestic oil is not enacted."[17] Thus, even when threats were made, they often went unheeded, or worse, served to distance the president from those who were meant to be the object of his persuasion.

Most of the threats recorded here were threatened vetoes. Given the president's institutional position with respect to Congress, this is not surprising; the veto is one of the few formal powers the president holds and one of the few clear-cut threats he can make. By constitutional design, the veto is supposed to give the president some leverage over the legislature, and the threat of a veto is intended to cast a large shadow over Congress. In reality, however, the threat carries little persuasive power and may be of limited utility to the president. Certainly, it will generate less leverage than the bargaining resources the president may exercise as a result of the vantage points that come with his position. Where presidential flexibility may commit a congressional representative to consider a presidential proposal more carefully, and where a well-placed favor may motivate a wayward senator to think about the president's position, the threat of a veto may easily float unheard through Congress or, worse, push others away. Persuasion rests less with the formal power of the veto than with the careful implementation of bargaining resources that do not fall to the president by constitutional design. Bargaining, not domination, is the domain of effective persuasion.

If presidents continue to threaten — and we can expect that they will — it may well be for the purpose of catharsis, not policy advancement. In a system of shared powers, there is little room for the president or any actor to impose his or her will. It follows that bargaining, not domination, emerges as the more efficacious process. But, bargaining does not always work and the president will not always get his way; this can be frustrating indeed for the chief executive with a lot invested in the outcome. I read the relationship between the use of threats and policy failure as a possible indication that presidents are more likely to rely on threats when they're in trouble, when they feel they are on the losing end of an initiative. Not all the threats were made during failed cases, of course, and not all came at the end, when the outcome often begins to become clear. But, threats do emerge more as a resource of last resort than as a primary means for persuading. Over time, they prove to be of limited utility, often ignored, at times having the opposite of their intended persuasive effect. But, it still must feel good to make them. Even if it does not put the president back in control, it no doubt makes him feel that he is, even if the feeling is unsubstantiated and short lived. If this is the case, presidents will still make threats, but they are not likely to advance their programs in the process.

CONCLUSIONS

When the use of presidential power serves domestic policy ends, effective persuasion plays an important part in advancing the president's agenda. But, motivational, not overpowering, persuasion moves others closer to the president's position. The power to persuade truly rests with the ability to bargain, to use in an effective fashion the resources of bargaining that bless the presidential office.

The president can bargain effectively, given his central vantage point in the Washington power structure and the resources of his office. Recent past presidents share a common pattern of using these resources during some of their major domestic policy triumphs. This is especially true of Presidents Carter and Reagan. They have generally managed to remain flexible and open to compromise, successfully convincing others that their willingness to bargain was a strength borne of a flexible nature and not a weakness stemming from lack of conviction, a tendency to vacillate, or a desperate reaction to circumstance. They have been able to use the considerable perks of the presidency as favors for others, especially those in Congress, in the process making the mechanism of bargaining work for them. They generally have avoided harsh words and instead chosen to operate in an atmosphere of rapport, which they facilitated through their words and actions. During their policy failures, these same presidents have used their bargaining resources less, and less well.

But the same vantage point that gives the president numerous bargaining possibilities makes it difficult for him to dominate. Persuasion through the force of threat is not effective, and possibly even counterproductive; persuasion through the pain of sanction is rare. Congress may easily overlook the threat, or accept it as real but not respond as the president would wish. With a distinct base of support and its own agenda, Congress is not in a position to succumb to presidential domination. Within the White House it is the same story. Vast and complex, the White House staff is far from an organ of the president and, as we will see in the next chapter, not organized with the president's wishes in mind. This will not stop presidents from making threats, but the reality of presidential effectiveness rests with motivation, not domination. Others in the policy system need to be given reason to accept a presidential perspective, be it the political or personal fulfillment of a favor, the psychological pull of rapport with the president, or the satisfying sense that the president is willing to meet one part-way. Bargaining generally succeeds where domination fails. But, as we will shortly see, neither is it the whole story of presidential power.

☆ ☆ ☆ ☆ ☆ ☆ ☆ ☆

Three resources of domination were examined for their relationship to presidential effectiveness. Of the three, only the application of pressure on other policy actors was systematically related to the policy achievements of Presidents Carter and Reagan. But, effective pressure can be generated as much through careful bargaining as through efforts at domination. The other two resources of domination, meanwhile, were not related to the outcomes these presidents achieved. Threats were made somewhat more frequently during the policy failures of the two presidents, but in most instances the threatening words were disregarded. Too few mentions were made of presidential sanctions, such as actual vetoes, to believe that these had an important influence on outcomes. Overall, persuasion is best understood as a function of bargaining with, not domination of, other Washington actors by the president.

FIVE

Organizational Efficiency

In the heat of battle over President Carter's comprehensive energy program, the House Democratic leadership was hard at work promoting the White House line. For its part, the president's liaison team did not do quite as well.

> As effective as the Speaker was, the White House was equally ineffective. When the proposal for a four-cent gasoline tax increase was unveiled by the House leadership, the Administration hemmed and hawed, withholding its support for most of a day and angering leading Democrats who saw no reason why the Administration should oppose the plan . . . and a questionable amendment concerning utility rates slid through by a 19-to-17 vote margin in the ad hoc committee, at least partly because Administration lobbyists were on the telephone trying to figure out what their position should be when the vote was taken.[1]

Hampered by an inefficient organization, Carter was unable to send a coordinated message to Congress and lobby effectively for his program. Mentions of Carter's internal problems were commonplace during the energy drive; lack of communication, internal disagreement, and uncertainty about the correct course of action were typical. Yet, it is all too easy to assume that such organizational problems plagued the entire Carter *administration*. In fact, they were characteristic of those instances in which Carter had trouble promoting his agenda. Although such may have occurred frequently, it was not the story all the time. As we will see, when Carter successfully maneuvered his way through the congressional thicket, he was aided by an organization that was evaluated for its operating efficiency—just the opposite of the haplessly ineffective organization that has since come to characterize the Carter presidency.

Nor is this the case for the Carter administration alone. During the Reagan administration's successful effort to win congressional approval for his version of the 1981 budget, the president's political team was "widely praised as well-organized, purposeful, attentive and usually ahead of the Democrats on tactics."[2] A brief sixteen months later, during an aborted effort to win support for the Dense Pack missile-basing scheme, the Reagan team failed to operate effectively, leading some observers to comment that "the shine is off"[3] the president's reputation as one who could control Congress in part through coordinated strategy.

These over-time differences in organizational efficiency were not lost on White House and congressional actors. Specific references to organization were recorded for each of the thirty-four policy cases studied, and mentions of efficiency were distinguished from references to inefficiency. Organizational efficiency was characterized by positive evaluations of the White House organization, including its ability to coordinate, organize, plan, or enact strategy; like-mindedness among the president's staff or between president and staff; and general references to being well organized and coordinated. Organizational inefficiency, in turn, encompassed references to White House inability or failure to plan, coordinate, and the like; serious lack of agreement within the White House; and poor execution of goals.[4] This is a large assortment of items to include under the organizational umbrella, but each is believed to contribute to the overall organizational effort, with real consequences for presidential effectiveness.

The composite picture of both the Carter and Reagan organizations is one of great efficiency during successful policy efforts and great inefficiency at times when the power of the president falls short of what is necessary for the chief executive to get his way. The data portrayed in Table 5.1 are best viewed as an aggregate picture of the organizational characteristics of these administrations during success and failure, as viewed by participants within the White House and on Capitol Hill. Though sketchy, they suggest two important things.

First, *the percentage of references to organizational efficiency varies with outcome*. Successful outcomes are associated with a high percentage of references to organizational efficiency, of the type just mentioned. Unsuccessful outcomes are associated with

Table 5.1. Mentions of White House Organization

	Carter		Reagan		34 Cases	
Total Mentions* of	Success	Failure	Success	Failure	Success	Failure
Efficient White House Organization (%)	65	10	79	2	77	11
Inefficient White House Organization (%)	35	90	21	98	23	89
Number	(40)	(83)	(80)	(55)	(179)	(256)

*Percent of mentions on the general topic. In the first instance, 65 percent of those commenting on White House organization perceived it as efficient.

extremely few references to efficiency. The aggregate perceptions of observers in Congress and the White House itself indicate that presidential domestic policy success is characterized by a different set of organizational conditions than those in effect during policy failure. During success, observers are more likely to notice agreement within the White House over the president's agenda and the best way to approach Congress. There are fewer allusions to internal divisions, and more references to the ability to coordinate and plan. When the president succeeds, his liaison apparatus is more likely to be praised and perceived to be operating smoothly, and he is more likely to appear to be in agreement with this subordinates.

Second, *the ratio of references to efficiency relative to inefficiency varies with outcome in a manner that suggests efficiency is not an absolute quantity.* For Carter and Reagan successes, the ratio of observations of efficiency to inefficiency is roughly 2:1 and 4:1, respectively. During the failed endeavors of both presidents, the ratio of references is better than 9:1 the other way. The inefficient organizations in place during policy failures are characterized by an utter lack of coordination and agreement. But the proficient organizations we see during policy success still attract a fair share of references to inefficiency. Disagreement, poor execution, and confusion may still exist, but these are more than balanced by frequent perceptions of the opposite. This understanding of efficiency allows room for confusion to exist, but not reign, and for internal disagreement to occur, but not without some form of reconciliation or smoothing of differences—or at least the appearance of such. The pattern of references to organization characteristic of Carter and Reagan successes supports the premise that dissent and disagreement, captured here by references to inefficiency, may indeed be healthy parts of a deftly run White House, as long as the means for resolution are also supplied. Likewise, procedural problems may occur in both the efficient and inefficient operation, but only in the former will corrections be noted.

This relationship between organization and outcome is worthy of further exploration. Presidential policy successes in the Carter and Reagan administrations appear to be characterized by a particular set of organizational traits that differ from those in force when the president fails. Remember that the measures used here are loose indicators of perceptions, and the data are presented in aggregate form, downplaying individual variations and, for that matter, disregarding an objective picture of presidential organization. In the aggregate, policy actors *perceived* the institutional presidency to be in disarray during times when the president could not attain his objectives; quite naturally, to the extent that impressions influence actions, this affected the way they approached the White House, with obvious consequences for the president's ability to act effectively.

Data on organizational efficiency were gathered for the twenty-six additional cases of success and failure from Johnson to Ford in order to provide a broader base for comparison. When the findings for all thirty-four cases are compared with the Carter and Reagan results,[5] the preceding observations are supported. Over time, domestic policy success is characterized by a degree of organizational efficiency not found in the White House during policy failures. This is the case even though administrations tend to earn lasting reputations for organizational style and ability.

Beneath these surface reputations lie interesting variations in the nature of presidential organization that undercut the lingering impressions fossilized over time into conventional wisdom. Perhaps more important, the picture of variation suggested here implies a potentially significant role for presidential organization in the exercise of power in the domestic realm. The findings raise several salient questions. What exactly *is* organizational efficiency, beyond the cluster of items discussed previously? If organizational efficiency is indeed a force in the exercise of power, how can the president harness it? To what extent is the organization of the White House under the president's control, and to what extent is it influenced by factors he cannot sway? The remainder of this chapter will examine the elements of organizational efficiency in greater detail. I will address the concept of organization as an amalgam of fixed and variable qualities, some beyond the president's control, others within his grasp only on good days, still others within his power to manage much of the time. To make these distinctions, a certain degree of artificiality is necessarily introduced, for, as we will see, there is a fair amount of interplay among the items to be addressed. Still, these qualities have their roots in the observations composing the aggregate findings presented in Table 5.1. Variations in organizational efficiency will be explained from this perspective, toward the goal of understanding the place of organization in presidential effectiveness.

FIXED CHARACTERISTICS OF ORGANIZATION

Any effort to harness the institutional presidency will be influenced by personal and institutional factors inherent to its operation. Underlying presidential success and failure is an organizational foundation whose support beams include presidential management style, the institutional constants of the contemporary executive branch, and the climate of expectations in which the president operates. These items are beyond the president's control, to be understood and accepted perhaps, but not readily manipulated. As such, one would expect their contribution to successful outcomes to be limited to defining the circumstances under which the president will attempt to make the executive branch work toward his ends.

I choose to approach the chief executive's management style as a constant factor in the organizational setting, even though, as a function of the individual president, it is subject to alteration at least in theory. I do so because presidents tend to feel comfortable with particular approaches to managing their environment, developed over the course of a lifetime as an aspect of their characters; scholars are correct when they view administrative styles as characteristic of entire administrations. As individuals, presidents are inclined to feel comfortable with particular cognitive styles or management methods.[6] Kennedy and Johnson employed what Greenstein refers to as a collegial style, creating an open system geared toward imaginative give-and-take among staff members. Eisenhower and Nixon, in contrast, were more formalistic.[7] And, where the latter was wont to build a ''Berlin Wall'' around the Oval Office through the likes of John Ehrlichman and H. R. Haldeman, Gerald Ford preferred the more open, flexible approach of Donald Rumsfeld and Richard Cheney.[8] Ronald Reagan continued to see himself as chairman of the board even after he realized that cabinet government was unworkable. Whereas his level of involvement varied from issue to issue, his overall approach to management did not. So, although he spent countless hours on the telephone in the spring of 1981 trying to change congressional minds, he nonetheless delegated the twin tasks of lobbying and policy development to subordinates. As president, Ronald Reagan chose to preside.

Jimmy Carter's style was substantively different than his successor's, but it was similarly consistent. Carter's White House was characterized by a high degree of presidential involvement coexisting with a sizable amount of bureaucratic disarray. Unlike in the Reagan administration, presidential goals were never clarified. Even though Carter was deeply involved in the details of legislation, his style did not allow keeping close reign on those he relied on to develop it and sell it to Congress. Although there were structural and personnel changes in liaison and policy development following the administration's rough start with Congress, the president's administrative style remained fixed.[9]

If one views the White House bureaucracy as an extension of the president, the importance of management style to executive organization is great. This, essentially, is Neustadt's position: the staff is a tool to be used by the president to cary out his agenda. It is a personal orientation to organization that sees the president in the middle of the organizational universe, shaping his surroundings (provided he is wise and capable) to maximize his influence. Alternately, one could take an institutional perspective and place greater emphasis on the attitudes, actions and agendas of presidential subordinates as they are distinct from and possibly contrary to the president's desires.[10] It is quite possible that the latter perspective is more fruitful for understanding how the president can manage to create and maintain an efficient organization, at the very least because it captures the complexity of the environment in which the president must work, more so because it more accurately reflects the significant place of others in the institutional presidency to define the parameters of authority from which presidential power may flow. As Greenstein asserts, "Leadership in the modern presidency is not carried out by the president alone, but rather by presidents with their associates. It depends therefore on both the president's strengths and weaknesses and on the quality of the aides' support."[11] I will argue that the president has some degree of control over several variable qualities inherent in the organizational setting of the White House, in which his actions may well affect his power to attain policy results. But the emphasis is on influencing those aspects of the institution over which he has some leverage, assuming the office is much less than an extension of its occupant.

This would naturally emphasize the institutional factors the president has to face. Even more than management style, these are a fixed part of the institutional environment. All chief executives since FDR have headed a swollen presidency, with thousands staffing the Executive Office of the President alone. The fifty presidential assistants advising FDR had increased in number by a factor of nine by the time Nixon left office. Furthermore, the occupants of these positions frequently leave for greener pastures. This occurs between administrations, and to an ever-increasing extent within administrations as well, making inconsistency and turnover one hallmark of the administrative setting. The large numbers are the outward manifestation of great specialization, of subunits staffed with individuals holding different, often competitive goals and objectives.[12]

Such diversity and specialization present the president with an organizational maze to navigate. We may treat this problem as a constant of his working environment, to be dealt with regardless of the momentary objectives the president wishes to achieve. These properties were present both when the White House was evaluated to be efficiently run and during instances of the opposite. It is likely that the nature of competition among subunits varied over time, across issue areas, and with the inevitable turnover among White House personnel. But it is unlikely to be related systematically to policy outcomes, given the complexity and breadth of both the successes and failures examined here. Policy successes like the Panama Canal treaty ratification fight, the 1981 budget, and natural gas deregulation did not naturally lend themselves to less in-fighting or internal conflict than did the energy program, Dense Pack, or other failed policies. Rather, the methods used by the president to harness the institutional presidency given its size and diversity are best understood as the qualities of organization that may account for differences in efficiency. These will be discussed shortly.

Complementing and perhaps complicating the internal status of the White House are the performance expectations placed on the president by the Washington community. Presidents may serve during periods in which Congress is aggressive and assertive or passive and receptive, just as they will inherit other political cycles and trends[13] or serve at varying points in the rise or fall of a political regime.[14] Like the institutional characteristics of the executive branch, these are emblematic of the environment in which the president must work, but it is beyond his control to do anything to affect them.

They determine the climate of expectations in which the president and his organization must function, which in turn influences the way Congress receives and evaluates the White House. The president who has to deal with a fractured coalition in Congress presents his organization a greater task than one faced with a Congress ready to tow the party line in response to strong congressional leadership. Carter faced the former situation, while LBJ initially faced something akin to the latter. If Congress is flexing its muscles, the president's organization may have a hard time bringing it around. According to Wayne, Jimmy Carter served with an aggressive Congress that had great expectations.

> The expectations of Democrats in Congress clearly exceeded the administration's capacity to fulfill them. ''Sixty percent of the Congress had never dealt with a Democratic White House, so they didn't have realities in mind,'' suggested a top liaison official in an interview. ''They looked for a rubber stamp White House. It was a learning process on both sides of the street.''[15]

Whatever mistakes the Carter White House made were evaluated against an extremely high standard, making it hard for the White House to come out looking good, especially as it worked through its early organizational growing pains. Conversely, the

Reagan administration took over a presidency diminished in the eyes of many by a weak president, with lower expectations providing the benefit of more operating room. As it happens, Reagan's congressional transition was "smooth and efficient";[16] still, he had the advantage of lowered expectations, a less assertive Congress, and out-party status that precluded the need to manage a fraying congressional coalition.

These items—especially the nature of the institutional presidency and the climate of expectations — may help explain why some administrations tend to have more success with Congress. They may help us understand why some presidents are perceived more frequently to run efficient organizations. But they do not explain variability in the perception of organizational efficiency within administrations. If congressional assertiveness colors aggregate perceptions of White House efficiency, this is a condition the president must live with over time. The institutional presidency will be no less vast, complex and Byzantine at the end of a term than it is in the beginning. Yet, perceptions of the way the White House is organized do indeed vary over the course of presidential terms, in a manner consistent with policy outcomes. If successful outcomes are associated with organizational efficiency, even during the administrations of presidents like Carter, who faced high congressional expectations and the usual burgeoning organization, the explanation must lie in other characteristics of the organization that are under the president's control.

VARIABLE CHARACTERISTICS OF ORGANIZATION

Five variable characteristics of organizational efficiency are displayed in the right-hand column of Table 5.2. Depending upon his skill and ability, the president may be able to work any or all of

Table 5.2. Characteristics of White House Organization as They Relate to Outcomes

Fixed	Variable
1. Presidential Management Style	1. Conflict Resolution
2. Institutional Characteristics	2. Coordination
3. Climate of Expectations	3. Capability
	4. Communication (Internal)
	5. Cooperation with Congress

these to his advantage and as such strengthen his organization as he pursues policy. As variable qualities, some or all of them may work for the president during a particular policy pursuit only to work against him during others. Especially as the arena of debate shifts from issue to issue, different executive branch actors are brought into the fight, and with them different possibilities for conflict resolution, coordination, and the other variable characteristics of organization to be discussed.

Conflict Resolution

One element of presidential management style is the degree of conflict tolerated or fostered by the chief executive. Legendary accounts of Franklin Roosevelt's White House show how a president can effectively encourage conflict among his subordinates as a vehicle for promoting ideas through the clash of differences. Other presidents, like Eisenhower and Reagan, preferred to operate in an environment of consensus.[17] Consider the different patterns of conflict resolution present in the following accounts of three presidencies. In the Eisenhower administration, cabinet meetings provided a forum for the discussion of issue differences.

> They were discussed with care and sometimes debated intensely, although Eisenhower made the final decisions and there was no voting. As well as being forums for debate, Eisenhower's cabinet meetings were occasions for bringing the debaters into agreement on the president's policies. And when not in agreement they were expected to close ranks once a decision was made, although slippage inevitably occurred.[18]

In contrast, differences among Kennedy aides tended to be resolved in a more free-wheeling manner. According to one assistant,

> Most of the time we just worked things out. Sometimes we would go out for dinner or lunch and hammer out some kind of compromise. There were times, however, when it came down to who carried the most weight. If you were a member of the strongest group, you got the most concessions. When a compromise couldn't be cut, the biggest coalition — no, the strongest coalition — would win. That was frustrating. Arguments didn't mean a damn if you were in the minority, unless that minority happened to include Jack Kennedy.[19]

President Nixon exhibited yet another form of conflict resolution, in which differences were managed formally by top aides. Said one participant, "Whatever else [John] Ehrlichman was, he was efficient. Along with [H. R.] Haldeman, [he] set up a tremendous system. The choices were handled with minimum conflict. If someone disagreed too frequently, there was a good chance that the someone would leave."[20]

Each of these methods of conflict resolution suited the president who promoted it, and each tolerated a different degree of conflict. Nixon's controlled procedures were designed to eliminate disagreement, Kennedy's openness, to tolerate it, and Eisenhower's group orientation, to resolve it. Absolute levels of conflict present in the White House at any given time depended in part on the tolerance level of the chief executive, as reflected in his management style. As such, the simple presence or absence of disagreement is not an adequate measure of organizational effectiveness, a contention supported by the data. Policy successes and failures were both characterized by some element of disagreement among the parties involved.

Successes are better distinguished from failures by the way conflict is managed. Policy success tends to be characterized by a favorable ratio of mentions of efficiency to inefficiency, in part capturing the greater likelihood that agreement will overshadow disagreement or that disagreements will be resolved. Regardless of the manner in which the president approaches conflict, relative agreement will occur only at times, to be affected as much by the nature of the debate and the contending personalities as the president's approach to conflict. Issue intensity and the individuals voicing opinions change with the arena of discourse, and these change the odds of agreement.

Issues fraught with factional politics obviously will be more contentious. But, factions may not form simply along policy lines. Light warns against viewing the president's staff as a monolithic entity, identifying cleavages that may form both between and within bureaucratic units. Thus, coalitions may develop not simply between, say, the president's personal staff and the Executive Office of the President, but within subunits. The House and Senate liaison staffs, for instance, could find themselves at odds over how to approach legislative strategy.[21] Such differences could be limited to a particular agenda item, or they might extend to deeper philosophical differences about how to approach the job.

The president can enhance his ability to manage some of these inevitable differences by considering the level of issue agreement and goal compatibility among his subordinates when making appointments. Once again, conditions in effect during the early days of the Carter and Reagan administrations are most instructive. Clear differences are apparent between the Carter and Reagan staffs in both the nature and extent of agreement on how to carry out the president's program. During the first several months of 1977, when President Carter was trying to win passage of his energy program, the president's staff was characterized by what Kessel calls a "chaotic issue structure," suggesting unpredictable diversity in the attitudes held by staff members toward policy. Kessel identified a spread of attitudes among top Carter appointees from Chief of Staff to legislative liaison officials, ranging from social liberal to libertarian, including an isolated attitudinal cluster that defied convenient labeling. Together, these individuals were charged with developing and selling the Carter energy package, but "to the extent that Carter staff members wanted to promote policies with their own preferences, it would be difficult to predict what they would do."[22]

In contrast, Reagan's staff was characterized by an extremely high level of agreement,[23] the result of a concerted effort to appoint subordinates committed to Reagan conservatism and loyal to the president personally. The inner circle of Reagan's transition team began the careful search for loyalists before the president was inaugurated, seeking to fill both major and minor White House positions with people whose past behavior suggested compatibility with Reagan's major program objectives. The effort included close, centralized staffing of the Executive Office of the President, key agency heads, and legislative liaison.[24] According to Nathan, as a result of these efforts, "Reagan's cabinet and subcabinet officials [were] ideologically in tune with their chief,"[25] providing a united front for Reagan's initial policy assault.

But careful control over the appointment process is only a partial solution to the president's problem of conflict management. People leave government, and an ongoing effort to identify and recruit replacements is an energy-intensive luxury more suited to the transition phase than to a working administration. More important, the 1981 budget case is the most salient example of Reagan's conservatism being brought to bear on the domestic agenda; if conflict management through control of the appointment process contributed to the administration's organizational efficiency, it yielded dividends in this specific instance, rather than during many policy contests on a host of issues over time.[26]

At best, the resolution of conflict is a variable matter that reflects changes in personnel and agenda. Over time, turnover in Carter administration personnel reconciled some of the divisions inherent in the early days, and as the agenda moved from energy to ratification of the Panama Canal treaties and natural gas deregulation, the administration was able to function more collectively.[27] Presidents can learn how to manage conflict, and how to adapt conflict to their particular management approach, just as careful manipulation of disagreement may be a useful strategy for coordinating some differences, but not others. Even giving the appearance of unity, as Eisenhower required, is a useful strategy only if the paper covering dissent is not too thin. Conflict management is a fleeting and imperfect art; if it is by necessity only an occasional characteristic of presidential organization, it is best employed during policy crusades that matter most to the president, when organizational efficiency can be used toward important legislative objectives.

Coordination

Closely related to conflict management in the design of an efficient organization is the nature and degree of coordination among the various actors working on behalf of the president. And, once again, the president's task is gigantic, requiring a commitment of time and energy that simply may not always be available. The swollen size of the White House staff is generally regarded as burdensome,[28] its many layers responsible for twisting or distorting the president's wishes. Whereas the president obviously has a vested interest in coordinating his legions, he alone among government actors is so inclined, yet he is far from suited for doing the job. As Heclo notes, by constitutional design, the president needs to organize an executive branch in which the president and department heads do not share political fates. As a result, "no public official short of the president has a vested interest in coordinating political management in the executive branch as a whole. But, by the same token no president has more than tenuous capacity himself to perform such a coordinating role.''[29]

As with conflict management, we would expect to find variations in the degree of coordination within the White House organization over time and across policy cases. The relative influence of different actors will vary over time, and different players will be introduced as the policy agenda changes. References to coordination within the White House include observations about who exercises influence and whether patterns of influence are centralized and clear. Policy successes are characterized by observations of explicitly organized and nonconflictive lines of influence as seen by those with both a White House and congressional vantage point. Confusion is the norm during policy failures. In each case, coordination within the legislative liaison operation and the influence of top White House appointees is paramount.

While Reagan was pushing his first budget through Congress, his agents were noted for being ''well-organized, purposeful, attentive and usually ahead of Democrats on tactics,''[30] and compliments about the effective ''nuts and bolts operation of his political team''[31] suggested machinelike efficiency. Such compliments bespeak a carefully coordinated organization with centralized lines of command from the top down and between liaison agents and the president's top advisors. Influence in the White House at that time was concentrated at the top around the triumvirate of James Baker, Michael Deaver, and Edwin Meese. Kessel finds that these three commanded respect and legitimacy from subordinates. Their central place allowed information about legislative options and potential political costs to flow upward through them to the president, and decisions to flow downward to liaison officers in a centralized manner. The fact that all liaison appointments had to be cleared at the top enhanced efforts at coordination and centralization.[32] Strategic decisionmaking was centralized around a top-level legislative strategy group and directives flowed downward to liaison personnel, who focused entirely on developing ties with Congress.[33]

This structure worked for a time, during which President Reagan experienced his early domestic victories. But, it is by no means the only way presidents have organized for success. Jimmy Carter's natural gas compromise was coordinated within the vice-president's office[34] along with an internally composed legislative liaison team. Vice-President Mondale relied upon his experience in Congress and his staff, in conjunction with Frank Moore and the liaison group. The liaison staff did not await directives from above, but functioned independently in a careful fashion: "At 8:30 every morning, the White House lobbying teams met in the East Wing office of Carter's congressional liaison aide, Frank Moore. There they plotted strategy for the day and then fanned out to appeal to anyone who could help: business executives, newsmen, [even] friends of Senators."[35]

A comparable effort was invested into winning support for the Panama Canal treaties, although in this case coordination originated within the upper levels of the president's staff. Starting, in the words of one top aide, " 'way behind the eight-ball,' " Carter's top aides in August 1977 "set up a task force headed by Hamilton Jordan, the senior member of the president's staff, to supervise getting treaty support."[36] The task force was used to set priorities and establish a singular direction for White House lobbying. It functioned in conjunction with legislative liaison and the recently established public liaison office to build support for the administration's position.[37] Unlike the formula used by the Reagan team, legislative liaison officials were drawn into decisions about policy and strategy. In this instance, the Carter method worked just as well. With the task force, legislative and public liaison working together, "the White House orchestrated a colossal public-relations and persuasion campaign that swung public opinion to roughly an even division on the treaties"[38] by early 1978, a far cry from the unfavorable spread of opinion months before.

Perhaps even more remarkable is the timing of the effort. While Jordan was organizing a Panama task force, the Carter administration was still reeling from the disarray and lack of coordination that characterized its failed energy efforts. At the very start of the administration, lines of authority were anything but clear, and it was hard to determine who was truly influential in moving the president's energy program. In sharp contrast to the Reagan White House, and even to its own operation in other policy areas, the influence structure was unclear. Symptomatic of the lack of coordination present at the time, a consensus did not exist over which officials wielded legitimate authority.[39] As a result, no one was fully in charge. The Energy Department's Assistant Secretary for Congressional Relations, Frederick P. Hitz, was unable to carry out his responsibilities effectively because "neither he nor Energy Secretary James R. Schlesinger . . . had consistent control over the Administration's energy strategy."[40]

To confound matters, the Carter White House was arranged in a manner that blurred rather than clarified lines of influence. Initially, legislative liaison personnel were left out of policy formulation, which was seen as the domain of the Domestic Policy staff. White House liaison personnel were not expected to have a grasp of policy specifics as long as they understood the politics of a matter. But liaison officials in the departments were involved in program development and did get involved at all stages of policy making, promoting their view of politics and policy and thus working at cross-purposes with White House liaison agents.[41] The reason for this apparent lack of coordination was the errant belief that White House liaison should be established around issues constituting the president's agenda, an approach corrected when it became apparent that it was a poor use of liaison personnel.[42]

Neither was the problem limited to liaison. At the highest reaches of the Carter White House, the absence of clear lines of influence resulted in the sometimes amazing lack of awareness between the proverbial right and left hands. When President Carter announced his politically volatile decision to fight a number of water resource projects close to the hearts of important members of Congress—at a time when his energy initiative was floundering—the Secretary of Agriculture did not have a say in the decision. In fact, Secretary Bergland "said he was not consulted: he learned of it from the news and was surprised, like almost everyone else."[43] Such was typical of the lack of coordination in the Carter administration during the early days of 1977.

Clarity of influence and clear lines of authority are common to the policy successes discussed earlier and absent from the failures. Although influence may be centralized at the top, it need not be, but for the president to coordinate his organization sufficiently, lines of influence need to be clear. The Reagan team worked most effectively by exercising tight control at the top; the Carter team never did. When the Carter organization was successfully coordinated during the Panama Canal and natural gas cases, there was a fair amount of interplay among bureaucratic units, an operation suited to the individuals involved. But when Carter failed, interplay deteriorated into formlessness.

Capability

Anyone who has ever worked in a group of any kind is aware of the importance of the capability of individual members to advancing group goals; not surprisingly, the same is true of the White House. The caliber of the people surrounding the president is an important determinant of how and how well the White House conducts business. But, to state that the president could improve the efficiency of his organization by encircling himself with competent people is to beg difficult questions about the meaning of capability and how to find it.

At the very least, references to organization that take into account the capability of the president's minions indicate where to look. Although a fair number of comments may be found about cabinet members and the president's inner circle of advisors, observers focus most heavily on the ability of the legislative liaison staff. Comments about White House efficiency made during policy successes tend to address the proficient nature of the people handling congressional relations; similar remarks made during presidential failures focus on the perceived inability of the liaison group. This is not surprising. Legislative liaison is the part of the president's organization most visible to Congress, on the front lines of legislative skirmishes and likely to come under close scrutiny at both ends of Pennsylvania Avenue.

As a result, it is of paramount importance that liaison personnel understand the institution of Congress, how it works, and how to relate to its members. One might think that such would be an obvious prerequisite for anyone the president would place on the liaison staff; the observations made during policy failure suggest otherwise. When it becomes clear to members of Congress and reporters that, after ten months in office, "a White House staff dominated by young Georgians is still trying to get a grasp on Washington,"[44] obviously something basic is missing. Light argues that the original Carter liaison operation failed to command a fundamental understanding of the legislative process, making it impossible for the Carter team to respond effectively to congressional needs.[45] The result of this failure was the widespread perception that liaison in the early days of the Carter administration was being conducted by amateurs who lacked the capability to move the president's agenda through the legislature. The president's energy proposals suffered as a result.

So extreme was Carter's initial difficulty that it nicely illustrates the importance of capability to efficient organization. As personnel change, the president has an opportunity to bring in new individuals more suited to liaison work—or faces the risk of weakening an effective liaison operation with less capable replacements. Thus, the overall level of aptitude will fluctuate over the course of an administration as the cast of characters changes. In fact, over the course of his term, President Carter made replacements in the liaison office, bringing in new people who were widely regarded to be more capable,[46] and some of the original members benefited from what amounted to on-the-job training. Although the memory of earlier ineptitude dogged the Carter team throughout, the later Panama Canal and natural gas successes were characterized by a rise in the number of favorable comments about individual capability.

This suggests a relationship between capability and experience, an association strengthened further by a comparison of the early Carter and Reagan encounters with liaison officials. During the transition from the Ford administration, President Carter appointed Frank Moore to be his liaison chief. Moore was a friend and assistant from Georgia who had served briefly as executive secretary to Governor Carter, a position that included maintaining relations with the Georgia General Assembly. But Moore had no Washington experience, and he was unable to ferret his way through the avalanche of congressional phone calls, messages, and requests that naturally befall the president's personal representative.[47]

Furthermore, in Atlanta, Moore had been a part of the "younger group" of Carter advisors, a circle of aides that included Hamilton Jordan and Jody Powell, who were able, devoted, confident—and inexperienced. This circle worked in tandem with a set of older advisors: pollster Bill Hamilton, public relations advisor

Gerald Rafshoon, and a "kitchen cabinet" of advisors including Georgia state Democratic party chairman Charles Kirbo. According to Glad, the older group provided an essential balance to the younger one. "They helped smooth the road for Carter in circles in which he did not have any support. Overall, they provided a mature perspective and depth in their advice, which could not be found in a young office."[48] Carter chose to select his chief legislative liaison officer from the younger group of less established and mature aides. Though able, Moore came to the White House lacking the experience so often necessary to mold raw talent into proven capability. He was still learning when he left Georgia for Washington.

In contrast, President Reagan filled the top legislative liaison slots with people whose capability was long established and obvious to observers, including scholars of the administration,[49] who noted their lengthy records of service in similar posts. As president-elect, Reagan established a separate transition liaison office, run by "an experienced congressional lobbyist, Tom Korologos, and consisting of eleven professionals including two former White House congressional aides. . . . Every member of the staff had some Capitol Hill experience."[50] Although Korologos did not stay on after the transition, he was replaced by Max Friedersdorf, a veteran of recent Republican administrations. Said Charles Jones, "It would be hard to imagine a better choice, given the circumstances. Friedersdorf served on the liaison team for both the Nixon and Ford administrations, and before that he worked for a House member from Indiana for ten years. He also served as chairman of the Federal Election Commission, an agency with many congressional contacts."[51] The people below Friedersdorf were also well steeped in Washington politics: Powell Moore, Reagan's first chief Senate lobbyist, had been a White House liaison officer for Nixon and Ford; Kenneth Duberstein, Moore's House counterpart, had worked congressional relations for the Department of Labor and the Social Services Administration; William Gribbin, Friedersdorf's deputy, had worked for the Senate Republican Policy Committee. All were experienced in the ways of Congress and understood the presidential-congressional relationship.[52] They were, in the words of House Speaker Tip O'Neill, "an experienced and savvy team."[53]

At the very least, prior experience is a good yardstick of capability, against which predictions of promise in present posts can be made with confidence. But although past experience may be a good indicator of capability, it is neither a substitute for nor a guarantee of performance. Presidents should evaluate candidates for liaison positions with care, because their ability will reflect on the entire organization. And they should be precise about what they evaluate.

The Carter and Reagan episodes suggest that both the *nature* and *amount* of experience matter. By the time he arrived in Washington, Frank Moore already had practice working with a legislature, but understanding the Georgia General Assembly did not translate into knowledge of the United States Congress. Max Friedersdorf and his main deputies were veterans of both legislative liaison *and* the Washington establishment, a particular mix of experience that prepared them for their White House tasks. They had already proved themselves in Washington liaison operations and were known to be capable. Instead of selecting from his circle of California advisors, President Reagan dipped into the well-established pool of Washington Republican regulars for these critical liaison positions. President Carter reserved liaison positions for his friends and long-time aides. The different results they achieved are indicative of the difference between staffing liaison with known quantities respected for their competence, and resting key programmatic responsibility in the laps of individuals whose prior experience was outside Washington.

Communication

Whether you care to see it as a group of individuals or as a host of individual groups, the White House staff is a complex entity. The immediate interests and agendas of its members are not uniform. The growth of the presidency over the past two generations has transformed what was once a small staff into an institution of considerable size, creating a climate in which staffers do not necessarily understand one another because they do not know each other,[54] in which specialization yields disparate goals among different subunits within the White House staff, in which individuals vie for influence and advance their goals regardless of the president's agenda.[55] As Light notes, "the goals of the legislative liaison staff may be different from those of the Domestic Policy Staff; the goals of the Council of Economic Advisors may compete with those of OMB.''[56] If the president is to harness the presidency for his own purposes, he must find a way to work amidst many different currents.

Under these circumstances, internal communication is critical to operational effectiveness. Even if the president is inclined to let differences flourish around him, and especially if the president is determined to reduce disagreement, it is critical that clear channels exist within the White House so that the staff has a way to find out what is going on. Communication is closely tied to coordination; it is necessary to it and reflective of it. Open lines of communication are prerequisite to an organization operating in equilibrium. When Secretary Bergland was not informed of the Carter cutback of water resource projects, it demonstrated a lack of coordination underscored by poor communication. But a well-established operation will exhibit fluid connections among its members. Coordination implies staffers are listening to each other; communication makes it possible for them to hear.

Three distinct types of communication channels are present in the White House, each important in its own right: within subunits, between subunits, and between subunits and the president. Both the Carter and Reagan organizations appeared to exhibit the first kind of communication, although there were instances during the energy drive in which communication lapses within Carter's liaison staff may have contributed to difficulty cooperating with Congress, as we will see shortly. On the whole, Kessel found members of the Carter White House communicated primarily with others in their own subunit, such that Domestic Policy staffers conversed mostly with Domestic Policy staffers, legislative liaison with legislative liaison, and so on. Similar communication patterns could be found in the Reagan White House, notably in liaison (which witnessed a smooth initial transition in leadership marked by close work between outgoing liaison chief Tom Korologos and incoming boss Max Friedersdorf[57]), the Office of Policy Development, and the Legislative Study Group (called the *dynamo* behind Reagan's early domestic policy victories[58]).

But where both administrations exhibited communication within bureaucratic units, the Carter administration, at least initially, was not established to facilitate dialogue between subunits. Kessel contrasts the patterns existing in the Carter White House, in which within-group connections were made in lieu of between-group dialogue, with those present in the Reagan White House.[59] During his first years in office, President Reagan's organization exhibited strong communication patterns both within and between subunits, with centralized coordinators forming the nexus of a communication network that flowed from subunits to the inner circle (Baker, Meese, Deaver) and back to the subunits.

Although Kessel did not attempt to relate these patterns specifically to presidential performance, it is noteworthy that centralized communication is characteristic of the period of time in which President Reagan experienced his greatest policy successes,[60] and that the lack thereof is typical of Carter's early period of difficulty. Thus, observations of the Carter administration's initial "ineffective decentralization of lobbying,"[61] of the "sometimes woundingly contradictory"[62] lobbying efforts that peppered the energy drive, are consistent with the administration's failure to establish effective lines of communication among subunits.

As the administration progressed, changes were made, and between-group communication of sorts began to develop. Although it may not have resembled the efficient hub-and-spoke model of the early Reagan days, legislative liaison did begin a dialogue that had been absent earlier with the domestic policy staff and the new public liaison office. Together, they were able to discuss a more unified approach to selling the Carter domestic agenda and to the legislative process in general, a change that was in place in time to work on the long-shot Panama Canal treaties.[63] As one Carter aide said of the change, "in the process of gearing up for a tough fight, we got organized, too."[64]

It is just as important for the president to be involved in White House communication as it is for messages to flow freely within and between subunits. Especially if the president hopes to manage the organization to achieve his ends, direct communication is of paramount concern. Presidential involvement, made possible by open lines of communication, can influence internal decision making, and as Congress perceives a particular endeavor to be an important part of the president's program, it can lend legitimacy to lobbying efforts carried out in his name.[65]

As governor of Georgia, Jimmy Carter was a willing participant in this type of openness, engaging in an ongoing dialogue with staffers.[66] But in Washington, especially during his early days, Carter tended to neglect similar communications. With a larger staff and a full slate of policy objectives, he focused his attention elsewhere, choosing to let his staff communicate in his absence. Especially in his treatment of liaison, his tendency, like that of Richard Nixon, was to consult little, leaving his staff to face Congress without his input—and, apparently, his endorsement.[67]

President-staff communication is also a two-way street should the president choose to permit traffic in both directions. Such was President Reagan's tendency. When Friedersdorf headed legislative liaison, the president was open to his input; Friedersdorf "could educate the president about all aspects of Congress and advise him about when and how to be involved."[68] This opened liaison to the president's ideas, opened the president to the experience of his subordinates and legitimated the liaison operation by giving policy a presidential stamp.

Cooperation with Congress

One critical quality that separated the initial Reagan and Carter liaison teams was knowing *how* to get along with Congress. The Reagan team, deep with veteran congressional operatives, knew how to approach Congress. The Carter team did not. At their worst, Carter administration efforts to reach out to members of Congress were almost comical, like this misbegotten attempt simply to get a senator to the White House:

> When [Nebraska Senator Zorinsky] went to meet the White House car at the corner of First Street and Delaware Avenue, no car appeared. . . . [Later] a White House liaison man came rushing in to explain that the car had been at the wrong spot and was now ready. He added, "The President is waiting to see you!" Zorinsky balked. . . . He was irritated by the mistake. "Another instance of White House inefficiency!," he snorted.[69]

Unimportant as this may seem, small things are indicative of the way people are treated. To Senator Zorinsky, the auto episode was an unnecessary interruption of a packed schedule, and another in a perceived line of failures to cooperate smoothly with Congress. What Zorinsky saw as inefficiency was the inability of the Carter liaison operation to meet congressional needs. It was the outward manifestation of a problem internal to the White House. Usually, the real difficulty has its origins in one of the problems addressed earlier. It is treated separately here because, as we will see, the way the White House approaches Congress is likely to be interpreted in terms of cooperation. Regardless of its roots, cooperation is best identified as an important outward sign of the efficiency of the president's organization.

In this case, the problem derived from ineffective coordination at a very basic level, and the difficulty was in execution, not planning. The Zorinsky car escapade occurred while the Carter administration was trying to build support for the Panama Canal treaties—a successful policy endeavor noted for its effective planning (recall that strategy was developed by a centralized task force). But regardless of how well lain the plans may have been, the administration was still troubled by occasional mix-ups like this as a result of poor coordination within the liaison office over nuts-and-bolts matters.

The problem was exacerbated by failures of internal communication. At the most simplistic level, this was obviously the case: someone gave the driver the wrong coordinates, or directed the senator to the wrong street corner. But, simple as the problem may have been, the Carter administration's failure to come to grips with it undermined other successful efforts at coordination. The White House had managed to restore order at higher levels, enough to coordinate a plan of attack for the treaties. But internal communication within the liaison office was still wanting.

Reduced cooperation with Congress could also stem from a lack of capability on the part of liaison operatives. Recall that one of the consequences of Carter liaison chief Frank Moore's inexperience was the inability of his office to stay on top of congressional phone calls, messages, and requests. Unfamiliar with the way Washington works and unprepared for the sheer volume of congressional input, Moore and his office were incapable of approaching Congress in the manner it expected. The resulting treatment was perceived by Congress as the uncooperative deeds of pompous outsiders. Indeed, part of the problem was rooted in arrogance and ignorance, as when the Carter administration attempted to block politically important water projects during the first months of his term. One enterprise in question was in the state of Washington, home of prominent Democratic Senator Henry Jackson. "One Carter aide, when told he should clear a [water] project with Jackson, asked 'why do we have to clear anything with Jackson? We beat Jackson [in the Democratic primaries].' "[70] The comment is naive and smug, the reaction of a novice lacking in Washington experience. Although a reflection of limited capability by Carter's operatives, it is hard not to view it as a case of subpar cooperation with Congress.

It is also possible that limited cooperation could derive from willful disregard of Congress by administration operatives, although one might think this is an unlikely possibility, even if the administration they represent holds a hostile attitude toward the legislature. President Reagan presented himself as the great foe of Congress, even as he was building an efficient liaison team in 1981 that would reach out to the legislative branch. Regardless of its public posture, no administration is likely to aggravate Congress intentionally, especially through the channels designed specifically to facilitate relations. If it were to happen, it would represent the one context in which the failure to cooperate is not driven by other deficiencies in the White House.

Either way, members of Congress tend to react to the problem rather than look for the cause. Whether cooperation is strangled by capability problems, by coordination failures, or even by design, it will be experienced as a barrier to smooth relations. One need only look at the way Congress reacted to instances where cooperation was not forthcoming to understand this.

Once again, the Carter energy project provides the strongest reactions. The real cause was not important when the House leadership criticized the Carter administration "for failing to provide expected support for leadership efforts to maintain the strength of the president's [energy] program."[71] What mattered was that the White House did not cooperate. Around the same time, when "Senators said they could not get concise and timely explanations from the administration for specific measures,"[72] they were reacting to the barriers they felt around the White House, regardless of whether they privately cared to identify their cause. When House

Republican Whip Robert Michel lamented, "we have been asked to wait for phone calls that never come and detailed briefings that never materialize,"[73] he was expressing the frustration of trying to work with an administration that, for whatever reasons, did not cooperate.

In an effort to understand these reactions more systematically, congressional evaluations of Carter and Reagan organizational efficiency were recorded. Whenever a congressional actor made a reference to the president's organization that included an evaluative component, it was interpreted and coded on the simple 5-point evaluation scale discussed earlier.[74] Only evaluations of the White House organization clearly attributed to congressional actors were recorded; this accounts for the relatively small number of observations portrayed in Figure 5.1.

Essentially, these observations capture aggregate congressional perceptions of the *effectiveness* of the Carter and Reagan organizations. I distinguish effectiveness from efficiency the same way that I distinguish what members of Congress perceive as cooperation from what may be causing the White House to act toward Congress in a particular way. The primary benefit of an efficient operation is an effective relationship with Congress; the major drawback of inefficiency is the barricade it erects to a smooth congressional relationship. Thus, effectiveness is a good measure of the worth of an efficiently run executive branch.

The Carter administration was noted predominantly for its organizational ineffectiveness; the Reagan administration, for its relative effectiveness. Although the Carter group was perceived to be at its most ineffective during policy failures, these were also the occasions that generated the most congressional response: there were thirty-three evaluations of effectiveness during Carter failures, compared with only five discernable comments during his triumphs. The same general pattern holds for the Reagan organization. Members of Congress were moved to comment most during Reagan victories, when the organization they evaluated was largely noted for its effective dealings. Indeed, there is only one recorded comment about the state of organizational effectiveness during Reagan's policy washouts.

This reflects the general tenor of organizational effectiveness during the two presidencies. Carter, given his vast initial problems,

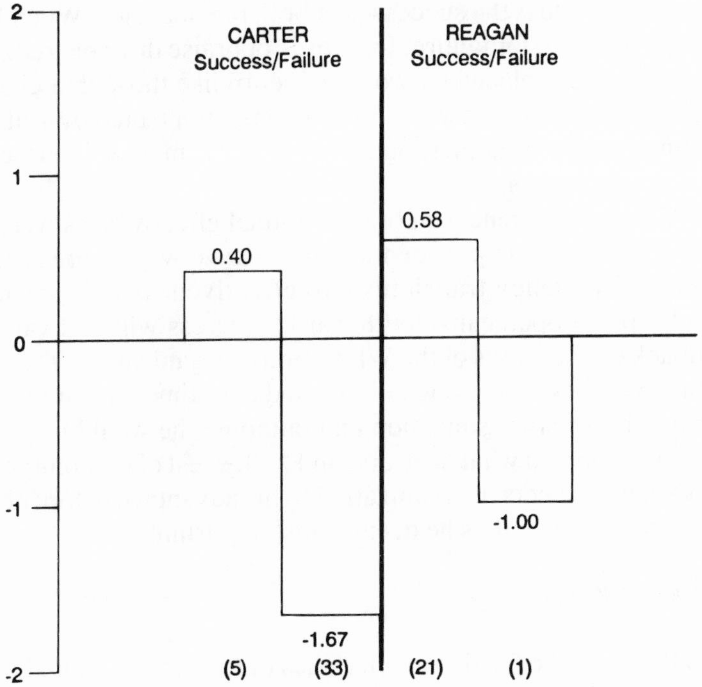

Figure 5.1. Congressional Perceptions of Organizational Effectiveness, Carter and Reagan

provoked stronger negative evaluations from Congress. Reagan, buoyed by his fast and efficient start, tended to draw positive reviews. But, Figure 5.1 bespeaks a relationship between organizational effectiveness and policy outcome common to both administrations. Although Carter's operation was generally viewed to be ineffective, such evaluations were most prominent during his failures. The average evaluation of the Carter White House during his two policy losses was sharply negative (−1.67). In contrast, the few evaluations made during Carter's successful efforts were, on average, rather positive (+0.40), more closely resembling the average associated with Reagan's successes (+0.58) than with his own failures.

Although more people volunteered comments when Reagan succeeded, the nature of those comments, on average, is strikingly comparable across the successes of both presidencies. When Reagan was destined for failure, the words of praise disappeared, perhaps not to be replaced by words of scorn like those that characterized Carter's failed escapades, but to be supplanted by a silence deafening to an organization noted for its remarkably effective ways at other times.

Clearly, differences in organizational effectiveness were not lost on Congress as presidential failure gave way to presidential success. Efficiency translates into effectiveness; the president who keeps an open ear tilted toward Congress will find valuable feedback on the status of the White House organization. The comments may vary from issue to issue and over time. Given the relationship between organization and outcome, he would be best to focus attention on what he hears, and to the best of his ability work the variable aspects of organization to his advantage before engaging in the policy battles he deems most important.

CONCLUSIONS

Between the fixed characteristics of the organization that the president inherits and the many variable items that could absorb his time, it would seem as though the goal of efficiency would require a herculean effort. Furthermore, "organizational efficiency" has been introduced as only one resource to be used for a larger objective — presidential policy accomplishment. If efficiency alone is such a complex task, one might ask how it could be established concurrently with even greater ambitions. The president is only one person with limited time, but he alone will press for his objectives.

Realistically, no president will be able to harness all elements of his organization at all times. But, one of the lessons of this project is that he need not do so, provided he sets limits on what he hopes to accomplish in office and focuses on his major priorities. As long as he is cognizant of the key warning signs of organizational difficulty, he need not involve himself with small organizational details when time could be better invested elsewhere.

The signs of efficiency are often easy to recognize. Perhaps one of the easiest for the president to notice — and to control — is the background of the personnel chosen to staff the legislative liaison operation. Of all the variable qualities of organizational efficiency, the capability of the people who operate in the president's name can be most closely regulated, at least at the highest levels of appointment. When President Carter handed the liaison apparatus to a fellow Georgian with no Washington experience and limited liaison experience, the problems were immediate and obvious. President Reagan, also a former governor, also a Washington outsider, reserved liaison for experienced Washington operatives skilled in the ways of Congress, whom he could trust to staff the office with other individuals of similar expertise. As an administration progresses and liaison suffers from the inevitable revolving door, Washington experience should remain a critical resume item for potential replacements. Carter eventually learned this lesson, but he learned it long after early impressions had been allowed to linger.

Other problems may not be as readily solved, but they are easy enough to identify, if one knows where to look. Congressional feedback about the state of White House relations is an excellent source of input about the status of the president's organization. If Senator Zorinsky cannot connect with a White House driver, obviously something is wrong somewhere; if the Senator reacts angrily to what he terms *another* case of White House inefficiency, it should be clear that this was not just an isolated incident. Congressional reactions constitute the best measure of White House organizational effectiveness; if the president is hearing what he would hope to hear, then he can be assured that his organization is efficient enough to operate in an effective manner. If not, then further examination is in order.

This could take the form of paying attention to the level of conflict in the White House, and to the degree of internal communication. Although presidents will vary in the extent to which they enjoy being surrounded by disagreement, no president wants his administration to speak with multiple voices.[75] If this occurs, the president may have a problem of conflict management, or communication, or both.

Some of these difficulties are inevitable in any organization at some point. They will change as personnel come and go, and will be of varying concern across different subunits. Not coincidentally, organizational difficulties vary over time like successful outcomes. To maximize his power, the president must first choose his battles. Then, to the extent that organizational efficiency will enable him to operate more effectively, he should pay attention to the warning signs of chronic conflict, crossed communication, and congressional criticism.

The interplay of organizational efficiency with other resources to this point has been only suggested. But, the discussion of organization makes clear the importance of organization as a home base of sorts from which the president can operate. In Chapter 6, I will address access between president and Congress as a possible card in the president's power hand. It should be clear how an efficiently run White House would facilitate a dialogue between the two, and how a badly disorganized White House could hinder and obscure discussion. Furthermore, such interplay provides the president with a forum for exercising the more personal of his resources, especially those resources of bargaining I indicated are related to the results he achieves. It will soon become clear that both organization and persuasion likely play important roles in explaining domestic policy outcomes. I will address this possibility in Chapter 7.

☆ ☆ ☆ ☆ ☆ ☆ ☆ ☆

Presidential power in the domestic policy realm can be understood as a confluence of personal resources, such as those employed to persuade, and organizational resources, designed to build a base from which the president can operate. *Organizational efficiency* is an umbrella term capturing several aspects of the institution of the presidency that may be controlled to a greater or lesser extent by the president as he attempts to achieve his legislative objectives. This perspective on organization assumes a large and complex staff of individuals who, far from being simple extensions of the president, maintain their own agendas and objectives that will not automatically serve the president. To the extent that the president can harness his staff, his organization is said to be efficient.

Some elements of organization are wholly beyond the president's control, such as the size and complexity of the White House organization, "macroevents" like the mood and partisan composition of Congress, the climate of expectations facing the president, and even the president's management style, which is fixed by character and experience.

Yet, aggregate evaluations of presidential organization show great variation within administrations between periods of success and failure. This pattern holds for the Carter administration, despite its reputation for wholesale inefficiency; for the Reagan administration, despite its reputation for just the opposite; and across all thirty-four policy cases dating back to the Johnson administration. The reason for sharp variations within presidencies is explained by changes in personnel over time and across subunits involved differentially in policy pursuits, and by changes over time in five variable qualities of organization over which the president may exercise a degree of control. These include the successful management of conflict (allowing for different presidential management styles that will tolerate or encourage different amounts of dissent); effective coordination of subunits; capability of personnel, especially in the liaison office, to be anticipated at the time of appointment by prior Washington liaison experience; clearly demarcated channels of information flowing within and between subunits, and between the president and surrogates; and the amount of cooperation perceived by congressional actors between the two branches. This latter item is the best external measure of White House effectiveness with Congress, which is perhaps the most important result of organizational efficiency; effective legislative relations foreshadow solid grounds for the persuasive exercise characteristic of the personal side of presidential power.

SIX

Access and Other Resources

The importance of organizational efficiency to presidential power was discussed in Chapter 5. Included among the elements of organization was internal communication among White House staffers and between the staff and the president. Communication is closely related to access, as the availability of communication channels to policy players enhances the likelihood for dialogue. In this chapter, the role of access in the exercise of presidential power will be addressed more fully. I will also discuss three resources that are not systematically related to outcomes and, as such, are not central to the exercise of presidential power: the use of charm, competence with the detail of policy, and hard work.

PRESIDENTIAL AND STAFF ACCESS

Although important in its own right, the benefits of internal communication may be found in the nature of the dialogue the White House is able to carry on with Congress, inasmuch as access channels between the branches depend on the ability of the White House to organize the messages it wishes to send. Communication is a tool of access, the way in which people in different offices exchange ideas. Communication assumes access, and access provides the groundwork for dialogue; it is the cable through which the message may flow. Whether the president is inclined to lay the cable speaks to his organizational style and personal proclivities, which for reasons discussed in Chapter 5 are unlikely to shift much over the course of his administration. However, I suggest that whether he is able to do so depends more on the extent to which internal communication is operational.

If I am correct, we should expect to find differences between policy success and failure in the extent to which congressional actors perceived the White House to be receptive to them. Greater overall access during policy success would be consistent with greater White House organizational efficiency and its open internal lines of communication. To examine this possibility, references to access between the White House and Congress were recorded for all thirty-four policy cases. All mention of contact between the president or his staff and Congress, in person, on the telephone, or in writing were recorded along with all references to the president not making such contacts by avoiding Congress, canceling meetings, refusing to return calls, and the like.[1]

The reality of the powers shared by Congress and the president necessitates that access channels exist between the branches. As Table 6.1 demonstrates, this is indeed the case regardless of the outcome a president achieves with a particular project. Even in a policy failure, better than seven in ten references to access illustrate that it was granted rather than denied. Overall, there were 1,398 mentions of access, of which 1,185 indicated it was granted. These figures are far greater than those associated with most other resources discussed here. Whereas this in part is no doubt a function of the visible nature of access, which makes references to it easy to recognize and code, it also speaks to the importance of dialogue in any executive-legislative relationship.

Even with the overwhelming tendency of the White House to grant access to Congress, there are differences in the degree to which it is granted that vary with policy outcomes. Policy failures are characterized by less absolute channels of access, by a greater tendency for the White House to block or deny access to Congress. During policy failures, twenty-eight percent of the references to

Table 6.1. Congressional Mentions of White House Access

Congressional Mentions* of	Carter		Reagan		34 Cases	
	Success	Failure	Success	Failure	Success	Failure
Access to White House Granted (%)	93	62	95	82	94	72
Access to White House Denied (%)	7	38	6**	18	6	28
Number	(319)	(229)	(364)	(237)	(811)	(587)

*Percent of mentions on the general topic. In the first instance, 93 percent of those commenting on White House access perceived that it was granted.
**Rounded.

access indicated it was denied or disallowed; although this is a relatively small figure, it contrasts with the skimpy six percent of references to access denied during policy successes. Whether this difference suggests anything meaningful depends on the sort of items noticed by congressional observers when access was denied and their reactions to these items. If policy failures are simply composed of a slightly greater proportion of routine meeting cancellations traceable to organizational inefficiency, then they may rightly be of little consequence to the outcome. More important, the severity of congressional responses to limited access needs to be considered; strong negative reactions would suggest a problem for the White House. These issues may be addressed with a closer examination of the responses of policy actors during cases of success and failure in the Carter and Reagan administrations. As we will see, policy failure was characterized by inconsistent access to the White House that often left congressional actors openly agitated. Specifically, two important types of access will be considered individually: between the president and Congress, and between the president's staff and Congress.

Presidential Access

Access granted by Presidents Carter and Reagan to congressional actors reflects the general patterns displayed in Table 6.1. During policy successes, both presidents were perceived to grant requests for access better than nine times in ten; during policy failures, access was less routinely available. Table 6.2 displays all references to access granted by the two presidents that could clearly be categorized as either access to the president or access to a member or members of the president's staff.[2] It shows that when President Reagan did not fulfill his policy initiatives, he granted access

Table 6.2. Congressional Perceptions of Presidential and Staff Access, Carter and Reagan

	Carter		Reagan	
Congressional Mentions of	Success	Failure	Success	Failure
Access Granted by the President	90% (179)	65% (101)	94% (263)	79% (139)
Access Granted by Staff	98% (119)	56% (41)	99% (81)	92% (55)

to congressional actors only 79 percent of the time (N = 139), compared with 94 percent of the time when he succeeded (N = 263). The case for President Carter was the same, and more so: during instances of failed policy, only 65 percent of the references to presidential access mentioned that such access was granted (N = 101), a full 25 percentage points lower than when he succeeded (N = 179).

The nature of presidential access was far reaching—encompassing everything from mailings to meetings — and, when both presidents succeeded, the effort was complete. Noteworthy is the similarity of the efforts undertaken by the two presidents, both in the things they did and in the totality of the undertakings. During the successful Panama Canal treaty ratification effort, President Carter personally kept in touch with Congress, and in so doing, was able to maintain an active dialogue. For example, in late August 1977, "to win backing for the new pact, the president sent every member of Congress a telegram asking for his or her support."[3] Two weeks later, he did this again, "noting that the canal treaty negotiators appeared near an agreement and urging senators to keep an open mind."[4] Around the same time, Carter "met with a group of influential senators" to discuss the treaties.[5]

Carter's natural gas pricing compromise was characterized by similar activities. In August 1978, the president met at the White House with "two Republican senators and two Democratic House members," nailing down a compromise that followed "eight months of negotiations, two months of drafting language and three weeks of haggling over the fine print."[6] Weeks later, Carter continued to maintain open channels of access to Congress as he attempted to sell the compromise to both houses by "inviting critics to the White House and personally appealing to them 'to put aside any reservations you might have.' "[7] Note how access facilitates persuasion; Carter used personal channels to "appeal" to congressional skeptics, to culminate a compromise. As one might expect, personal access affords the president a pathway for the use of important personal resources.

When President Reagan achieved his 1981 budget triumph, he too invited congressional actors to partake in interpersonal dealings. Typical of his involvement was the flurry of activity that occurred on and around June 26, 1981, when "The president placed calls to sixteen Democratic members of the House last night and this morning. At least some of the members were phoned twice, and some were called off the House floor minutes before [a key budget] vote took place in Washington."[8] As with Carter, personal access was the vehicle for presidential persuasion, and it was widely used. The extent of Reagan's availability to Congress is well documented. Jones suggests that Reagan's "communicator-in-chief" style required maintaining open passages with Congress: "Although not from Capitol Hill, Ronald Reagan demonstrated respect for the politics practiced there. Whereas he was unlikely to be as close to the members as either Presidents Johnson or Ford, still he would not make the mistake of distancing himself from Congress in either thought or deed."[9] But the period of time of which Jones speaks is the early part of the first term, when President Reagan was holding White House breakfasts with bipartisan congressional leaders, when the director of legislative liaison said of Reagan, "we had to lasso him to keep him off the hill,"[10] — and when the president was stacking up impressive legislative victories.

Both Reagan and Carter policy failures were characterized by strikingly similar limitations in presidential availability to Congress, an observation supported by the data and better understood by examining specific remarks. In the spring of 1982, President Reagan engaged in an unsuccessful effort to hold the line on taxes, which culminated in a midyear tax hike. Despite bipartisan congressional urging for access to the president to discuss the budget, Reagan held firm; the only use for a lasso during this period would have been to deliver the president to the Capitol: "For ten weeks, President Reagan steadfastly refused to become personally involved in increasingly urgent bargaining between the bipartisan congressional leadership and White House officials on a compromise [on the budget]."[11] The president's reluctance to grant personal access to Congress extended to a refusal to mobilize his own liaison officers to fight his battles. In late May, following four days of voting in which Congress could not agree on a budget package, one observer attributed the stalemate in part to "the President's inability, or unwillingness, to step into the fray and whip his troops into line. He made some phone calls to wavering lawmakers, and a few statements at press conferences. But when the final vote approached, the President went to California for a vacation, not to the television studio for a broadcast.''[12]

It could hardly be inability that kept the president away, given the degree of access he had granted only a year before, during his successful push for a budget package in 1981. More accurately, the president had decided not to get personally involved in this one, a decision that appears not to have helped his cause. Although we are not in a position at this point to make a statement about the relative importance of personal access to other resources as they relate to outcomes, it is interesting to note that just three months later, in August 1982, President Reagan reversed himself on the issue of taxes and came out in support of a tax increase. This time he opened the doors to the Oval Office widely, and he got results—which could not be attributed solely to his change of position. As his friend Nevada Senator Paul Laxalt said of Reagan's midsummer push for a tax increase, ''This is the most difficult legislative challenge this president has had to face. It's tight as hell!''[13] But, following a campaign marked by presidential availability, Reagan succeeded. One White House aide called the president's campaign ''the most prodigious personal effort of his presidency.''[14]

Like Reagan during his failures, President Carter was wont to exclude Congress from his dealings, although his lapses were more likely to be attributed to ignorance than will. This assessment was given currency by Carter himself, who acknowledged in the wake of his energy program debacle certain omissions of courtesy and protocol, ''such as the failure to consult Democratic leaders as well as two committee chairmen on an emerging natural gas bill.''[15] Regardless of the reason, the result was limited access to the president. Speaking of the situation in force during the energy battle, Senate Majority Leader Robert Byrd recalled persistently urging a president of his own party to consult more with Congress. By mid-1977, with the president's energy program still on the ropes, Byrd said that the access situation had ''improved,'' but there was still ''a problem of no little significance.''[16]

These examples demonstrate the two-way nature of access channels, which makes them so important to the presidential-congressional relationship. Congress expects the president to make a personal effort to consult and inform, as well as to make himself available to those who wish to speak. During all policy cases examined here, this was the case to a great extent; neither Carter nor Reagan ever attempted to be an island. But during policy successes, access was granted to the greatest possible extent, during the Carter and the Reagan years. When both of these presidents realized their objectives, they rarely made themselves unavailable to Congress.

Staff Access

Like personal access, pathways for communication between the president's staff and Congress were wide open during Carter and Reagan policy successes. The figures in Table 6.2 indicate an even higher percentage of references to access granted by the president's staffers than by the presidents themselves—98 percent for Carter's staff (N = 119), 99 percent for Reagan's (N = 81). Some of these contacts were routine and expected, like appearances at hearings. Others represented the work of legislative liaison, which Light points out is responsible for negotiating the congressional environment by establishing lines of communication.[17] Still others indicated receptivity on the part of staff members, even at the highest levels, to congressional contacts. In early 1981, for instance, Reagan's aides made a point of keeping their doors open to key members of Congress, prompting House Speaker Tip O'Neill to recount that if he had a problem with the administration, he could "call the White house, where Mike Deaver or Jim Baker or somebody else on the President's team would always straighten things out."[18] Regardless of the source, the effort by both the Carter and Reagan staffs was total.

The picture of staff access during policy failure is less clear, as the two administrations differ in the degree to which they were perceived to be open to congressional contacts. Consistent with the state of access to President Carter during his policy failures, only 56 percent of the references to staff access indicated that the Carter people were open and available. This level of response is consistent with an administration that suffered from some of the organizational woes discussed in Chapter 5. It is the type of reaction that would lead one to believe that the state of staff access, like personal access, is related to the results the president achieves.

In fact, it appears that during Carter's misbegotten policy endeavors, closed lines of communication between Congress and the president's staff contributed to presidential distance in creating an overall picture of a detached administration. Observations made during the energy drive are replete with suggestions that "grumbling about inadequate consultation" came from multiple sources: "Congress, other departments, and even the senior White House staff."[19]

Many complaints about limited access derived from the closed manner in which the Carter staff planned the energy policy, which "miffed" the congressional leadership "because it was bypassed by the President's chief energy aide, James R. Schlesinger, when he sent the first energy bill to Capitol Hill."[20] Schlesinger and his aides were criticized for working "as if they were a self-contained unit," on a task "as hush-hush as the Manhattan project."[21] It was a style remarkably similar to that exhibited by the president himself:

> The process by which the President produced the energy proposal . . . reflected a detached, almost apolitical attitude that is alien to a capital in which self-interest is a fundamental precept of leadership. The plan was conceived in secrecy by technicians, challenged in haste by economists and altered belatedly by politicians . . . Mr. Carter entrusted the draftsmanship of his most significant domestic policy thus far to an aloof, intellectual Republican, James R. Schlesinger, who had firm convictions about energy goals but a minimal feel for political realities.[22]

But the problem went far beyond one individual. Rather, Schlesinger's methods typified the state of staff access during Carter's failed policy pursuits. In time, Carter learned of the importance of staff access, but he wasn't always able to get his subordinates to go along. Seven months after the Schlesinger difficulties, the situation was much the same: "Administration officials have been conspicuously absent on Capitol Hill in recent weeks, the President's pledge to become more involved in the energy legislation notwithstanding."[23] And, even when the president's staff managed to remain open to congressional input, it had trouble doing so consistently. Even when Carter's aides "mounted an extensive campaign" in April 1977 "to painstakingly explain to members of Congress the administration's upcoming energy message," their actions "contrast[ed] sharply with the Administration's handling of another major issue—the decision to eliminate a number of water projects. In this case, legislators were piqued that the action was taken without advance knowledge.''[24] Indeed, ''on the ... water project issue ... the White House does not seem to have worked diligently to find powerful congressional allies.''[25]

It would appear, though, that the problems of the Carter staff were idiosyncratic to the administration of the Georgia Democrat, contributing, no doubt, to his problems but not indicative of the nature of staff access during policy failures in multiple administrations. After all, the Reagan staff was highly regarded for its availability during policy successes *and* failures alike. As a result, policy failure cannot be characterized by conditions of limited access to the White House staff in systematic fashion across administrations.

However, even accessible administrations can be ineffective in their intent. Making possible the conditions for a dialogue with Congress may be necessary to achieving communication, but it is not a guarantee that give-and-take will come about, no less that whatever talks emerge will lead the administration toward its policy objectives. This may be what happened during President Reagan's failures. Congressional evaluations of the effectiveness of their contacts with the president and his staff were noted and recorded on the 5-point evaluation scale. All indications that contacts with the president or presidential surrogates moved an individual closer to or further from the president's position were recorded.[26]

In some cases, it was difficult to distinguish evaluations of the contact itself from evaluations of what happened once the contact was—or was not—established. Thus, to an extent Figure 6.1 addresses evaluations of the cable and the message. It is not surprising, then, to find sharp differences between success and failure in aggregate evaluations of both personal and staff access. These differences apply to both Carter and Reagan — during their successes, evaluations of both personal and staff access were largely positive; during their failures, personal and staff connections with Congress were perceived to be largely ineffective. As access facilitates bargaining, this lends additional support to the importance of the personal side of presidential power. But, to the extent that the contact itself is being evaluated here—and in many instances,

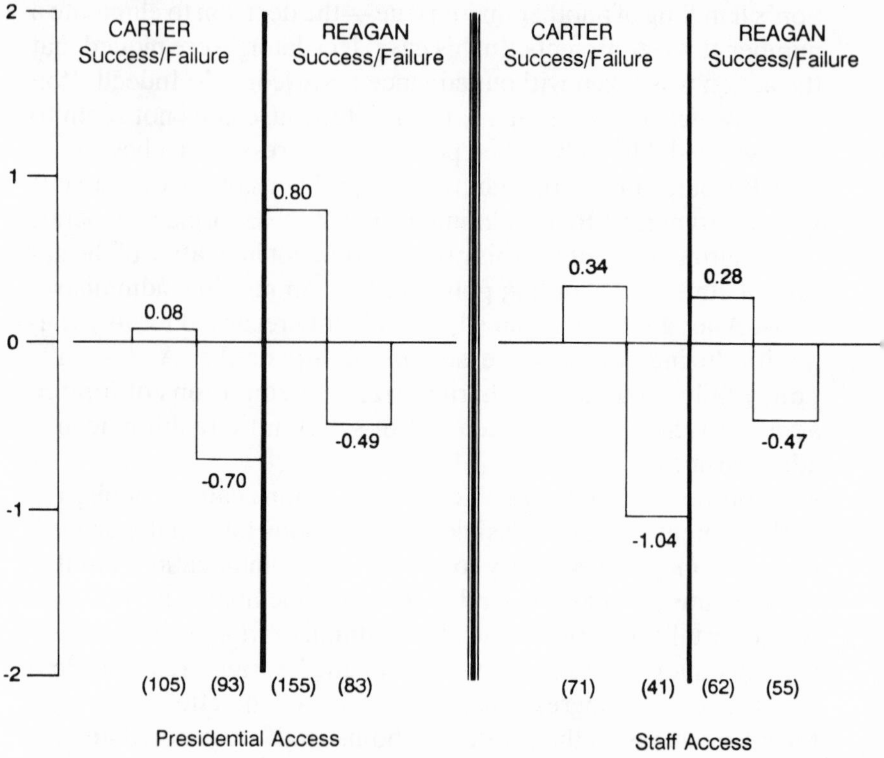

Figure 6.1. Receptivity to Administration Access, Carter and Reagan

such as the ones discussed later, evaluations of the contact are clear—it further supports the importance of access itself to making persuasion possible.

Whereas Reagan's team was perceived to be largely accessible during policy failure, it scored poorly (−0.47) when evaluated for its effectiveness. Like the Carter team during his policy failures, the average evaluation was negative (although, at −1.04, Carter's organization ranks at a different order of magnitude). I offer that the reasons for these negative figures are somewhat different. Carter's organization was criticized by Congress for its lack of access; in this light, the strongly negative rating is understandable. But, the Reagan team, as we have noted, was quite accessible. The negative evaluation, then, addresses not what was missing but what was not working.

During policy failures, the Reagan staff was perceived to be quite accessible but largely ineffectual. It is possible that congressional actors felt their dealings with staffers were not fruitful; it is not likely, given the high degree of contact they had with the staff, that they would have wanted more. Furthermore, the reasons for ineffective contact could have their origins in a sour congressional mood, in the staff's own internal difficulties, or both. During the 1982 tax initiative, President Reagan not only distanced himself from Congress, but from his own operatives as well, limiting communication with the liaison staff as he refused to get directly involved. Consequently, internal lines of communication between the president and his aides acquired static, hindering the ability of the Reagan operation to function smoothly. As discussed in Chapter 5, internal communication between the president and his subordinates, especially in liaison, is critical to effective dealings between the president's organization and Congress. Without it, access to Congress could be expected to be less fruitful.

If Congress was reluctant to accept the Reagan staff, the behavior of the president himself could have had a direct effect as well. Quite possibly, the negative evaluation of Reagan's staff was a backlash from the restricted personal access allowed by Reagan during his policy failures, which itself was met by congressional participants with a negative response (−0.49 on the effectiveness scale). I base this on the tremendous importance placed on personal access by Reagan during his successes, and the stunningly positive response that access generated (note Reagan's effectiveness score of +0.80). Recall that the successful cases happened first. After being treated to a long period of presidential access in 1981, Congress would not be expected to take kindly to the opposite treatment during the tax and MX issues of 1982.

To get a better sense of the contrast involved, consider the response to Reagan when he succeeded. Observers put a lot of faith in the president's simple presence. During his successful budget initiative, political leaders credited Reagan "with having earned political good will with extensive private meetings with Democratic as well as Republican leaders."[27] One chief foe, the Speaker of the House, said kindly, "The President has extended himself to members of Congress in a manner that is greatly appreciated by those who will be considering his proposals."[28] They are words he rarely said about Reagan's Democratic predecessor. In the end, "both allies and adversaries credited the president's personal lobbying with tipping the balance [toward the budget proposal]."[29]

President Carter never made this type of impression on Washington observers; even when successful, the impact of personal access to Carter was only marginally positive, as denoted by a mean effectiveness score of +0.08. In failure, when personal access was harder to come by and staff access was frustrated by organizational inefficiency, it is not surprising to find sharply negative evaluations (−0.70 for presidential access, −1.04 for staff access). Clearly, congressional actors did not take kindly to the restricted access they faced. Sometimes, the complaints were kept quiet, as when the White House lobbying efforts for the energy program "were privately criticized in House leadership circles for failing to provide expected support for leadership efforts to maintain the strength of the president's program."[30] Other times the comments were made in the open. But, they mark a striking contrast to the evaluations of president and staff heard when Carter triumphed, when a "desperate personal appeal" by the president swayed "two recalcitrant congressmen to pry loose the natural gas pricing bill,"[31] when "only Carter's personal intervention prevented [a compromise on natural gas] from collapsing."[32]

Still, the data imply that availability alone is not commensurate with effectiveness. *Lack* of access can only hurt, but availability of president and staff are no guarantee of results; personal and staff access are conditions of policy success, but they are not sufficient conditions. Of course, as far as access itself is concerned, a president or his staff can do little more than to make it available. Having done so, the emphasis must shift to the way it is used, to the tools of bargaining the president can apply directly or through his surrogates.

As the evaluations of Reagan's staff suggest, effective congressional operations exist at the juncture of access and activity, a product of an organization efficient enough to grant access regularly and effective enough to make it count. As the evaluations of presidential access suggest, effective congressional relations stem from the inclination of the president to make himself available, to know which personal resources to exercise when he does so, and to use these resources effectively. When Reagan realized his 1982 tax legislation, he was credited with having used an effective "personal sales pitch,"[33] emphasizing both the president's persuasive ability and the delivery system — personal access — that made it possible.

UNRELATED RESOURCES

Before considering a model of presidential power that includes the items discussed thus far, it is worth looking at additional data from the Carter and Reagan cases to examine briefly three resources that, like those associated with dominance, are not systematically related to policy outcomes.

Charm and Charisma

Hard to define and harder to measure, the associated concepts of charm and charisma are largely considered to be of great value to presidents.[34] Though intangible, presidential charm is at times the subject of comment, and I draw upon such overt references in developing a measure of its "use." Actors having contact with the president may make reference to the fact that the president was smooth, engaging, or magnetic. Or they may comment on the opposite: that he came across as unappealing or coarse. The greater the ratio of positive to negative references,[35] the greater the president's personal appeal.

A deeply personal characteristic, charm is unlikely to vary from moment to moment: a person is either charismatic or not. Unlike organizational efficiency, which can be improved with careful effort, or bargaining, a skill that can be learned, charm and related effects will not suddenly appear midway through a president's term. Results of the approximate measure of charm and charisma employed here tend to support this claim for Presidents Carter and Reagan. Although very few concrete references to charm or charisma were uncovered overall, the number associated with Carter was negligible both in absolute terms and when compared with the somewhat greater number of references to Reagan's charismatic abilities. Overall, as Table 6.3 attests, there were only seven references to charm during the four Carter cases, forty-five during the four Reagan cases.

Table 6.3. Mentions of Presidential Charm and Charisma, Carter and Reagan

	Carter		Reagan	
Total Mentions of	Success	Failure	Success	Failure
Presidential Charm and Charisma (%)	0	71	97	100
President Lacking Charm and Charisma (%)	0	29	3	0
Number	(0)	(7)	(33)	(12)

Most of these references were positive; that is, if the president behaved boorishly, policy actors were unlikely to comment on it, at least in a situation where their words could end up in print. Ronald Reagan, whose easy nature was well publicized, was attributed with forty-four positive references overall, a figure close to 100 percent of all mentions. Jimmy Carter was not universally known to be as smooth as his successor in one-to-one dealings, and this may be reflected in the smaller number of overall references to his charm. Still, most of these comments are positive as well.

Most interesting, though, is the distribution of these observations across policy cases. If President Reagan was indeed considered to be charming, this held for times when he succeeded as well as when he failed. Said House Speaker O'Neill of his political rival: "He's tremendously disarming. I just like him . . . as an individual, I think he's terrific."[36] But, if charm aided Reagan during the 1981 budget drive and the subsequent tax hike initiative, it was unable to bail him out of a failed effort to hold the line on taxes in 1982 or to win support for the Dense Pack basing scheme for the MX missile. Likewise, Jimmy Carter failed in his attempt to construct a comprehensive energy program even though the few, mostly positive references to his charm and charisma occurred while he tried. During both Carter successes, not one reference was made to charm, indicating that, at least as far as public record was concerned, it was not of prominent importance to other actors.

The most careful conclusion is that charm, charisma, and related personal attributes in and of themselves are not likely to be related to the result the president achieves. That is to say, charm is not of high priority in the network of presidential power resources.

President Carter can succeed while whatever charm he brings to interpersonal encounters goes unmentioned or unnoticed. President Reagan can be just as engaging when he fails as when he triumphs. The data do not support a direct relationship between charm and outcomes.

Where charm may be useful, however, is in facilitating the utilization of other resources, which are related to outcomes. Bargaining, for instance, is likely to be promoted by presidential charisma, which is one reason why some viewed President Reagan as "perfectly suited for a role that puts a premium on personal appeal and persuasive ability."[37] The more charming Reagan was better able than his predecessor to generate rapport with others. Personal charm may help the chief executive convince others that changes in direction come from strength, enabling him to employ flexibility to his advantage.

Whereas all of these are possible, they speak predominantly to the art of exercising power. Charm and charisma may be useful in cultivating that art for the president who can draw upon them. But in terms of advancing the agenda, charm apparently is not necessary and certainly is not sufficient. It is more a supplemental luxury for the president who is fortunate enough to have it and who is able to use it to complement his bargaining effort.

Expertise

Expertise as examined here applies to agility with the details of policy, to the president's grasp of the facts of the program he is pressing. It includes facility and accuracy with information, ability to grasp particulars, competence with the details of policy. It speaks to the president's knowledge of the specifics of his agenda. Expertise is demonstrated through mentions of the president's accurate use of information, his grasp of detail, his depth of understanding of policy specifics. The opposite, a demonstrated lack of expertise,[38] occurs when policy actors note the president fails to understand or comprehend the particulars of his own program or when he misuses facts and figures.

If Reagan was the more charming of the last two presidents, Carter was largely regarded to be the more technically competent. The attention that President Carter gave to detail is widely documented and probably as well known as his successor's lack of interest in specifics. But the data in Table 6.4 detail the limited impact this had on the results both presidents achieved. President Carter's superior grasp of information was acknowledged by others, and the highest percentage of mentions of expertise occurred during his policy successes, when 87 percent of fifty-two references mentioned the president's proficiency with detail. However, the corresponding figure for President Reagan is 42 percent of fifty-nine mentions of expertise, a number that suggests a rather limited grasp of the details of the programs the president would nonetheless effectively move through Congress.

Consider the following: "The president is said to have a detailed grasp of energy issues that sometimes impresses even the specialists."[39] The president being discussed is Carter, and the reference is to his ability to understand the minutia of his doomed energy program. In fact, specific occurrences support this observation, such as the president's behavior on a panel he attended with West Virginia energy producers during his third month in office. "Mr. Carter seemed to have been well briefed for his appearance on the panel. At one point in the discussion, he asked Allen T. Hamner 3rd, a chemistry professor at the University of West Virginia, to compare the BTU potential and sulfur dioxide content of coal produced here in Appalachia and that mined in the Western United States."[40]

In sharp contrast, Ronald Reagan's "command of details was slight,"[41] even during his successful 1981 budget drive. His lack of substantive answers to questions of policy stood "in marked contrast to Carter, who always had facts ready."[42] "Even the president's most loyal backers acknowledge that he does not have the detailed command of issues exhibited by predecessors Richard Nixon and Jimmy Carter."[43] Through policy success and policy failure, the president was regarded to be light on factual understanding. These comments were made early in his first term, when

Table 6.4. Mentions of Presidential Expertise, Carter and Reagan

	Carter		Reagan	
Total Mentions of	Success	Failure	Success	Failure
Presidential Expertise (%)	87	54	42	36
Presidential Lack of Expertise (%)	13	46	58	64
Number	(52)	(57)	(59)	(45)

he was having great success with Congress. They continued during less favorable times; the 1982 State of the Union address, delivered while President Reagan was attempting unsuccessfully to hold the line on taxes, was roundly criticized for being "shot through with errors of fact."[44] One White House staffer called the speech "his [Reagan's] worst ever."[45]

The pattern that emerges is the reverse of what we find for the use of charm and charisma. Although President Reagan could be considered charming and charismatic even in failure, he could be viewed as having a fixed and narrow appreciation of the details of policies even when he succeeded. But, whereas the patterns are opposite, the conclusions about both resources are the same: like charm, expertise is of limited value as a power resource. Carter was not able to better his cause because he had it, and Reagan did not suffer because he did not. In fact, to the extent that President Carter invested so much of his energy in developing his knowledge of policy specifics, he may have damaged his chances by placing so much stock in the wrong power resource. Conventional wisdom may claim that knowledge is power, and in fact other *forms* of knowledge—of how to bargain and organize—do strengthen the president's hand. But knowledge in the form of policy specifics is of less value to the president who hopes to use power to realize policy objectives.

Initiative

Of the two presidents, Jimmy Carter was the harder worker, although the data presented in Table 6.5 suggest the disparity with Ronald Reagan was not as great as conventional wisdom might suggest. Initiative was captured by references to the amount of time and energy the president invested in his job, specifically as that investment promoted the policy case at hand. References to the president keeping short hours or not putting in the effort to foster his

Table 6.5. Mentions of Presidential Effort, Carter and Reagan

	Carter		Reagan	
Total Mentions of	Success	Failure	Success	Failure
Presidential Hard Work (%)	93	83	70	67
Presidential Failure to Work Hard (%)	7	17	30	33
Number	(55)	(54)	(81)	(18)

policy interests are taken as indications of presidential failure to work hard.

Overall, 88 percent of the references to Carter's effort mentioned he was a hard worker; the figure for Reagan is 69 percent. Once again, there is little difference between policy success and policy failure for either chief executive. Carter's effort was only slightly greater during his successes and great all around. Reagan's was moderate when he succeeded and when he failed. The picture of Carter as a hard worker is consistent and clear. "'He's very much an activist,' one aide said" during the early days of the administration.[46] Later, even as he struggled with his energy program, the president's schedule remained "strenuous,"[47] his effort "vigorous":[48] "Typically, the president pushed himself even harder than he did his aides."[49] It was much the same story when Carter succeeded, as he did with the Panama Canal treaties, when "even those who know his capacity for work" were "amazed at the energy and effort" he devoted to the drive.[50]

Reagan's efforts were more tempered. Although he was perceived by aides to spend "long hours" in the office discussing budget options in 1981,[51] he was also one to keep "a tight schedule" that "spurns long hours in the office."[52] Where the president "worked very hard on his budget, using his staff, the telephone and television to hold the Republican party together,"[53] he was also seen by some as a bit removed. "Not since Dwight D. Eisenhower left the White House two decades ago had the United States had a leader so deliberately detached from the day-to-day hurly-burly of Washington as Reagan."[54]

But if time and energy as raw qualities are themselves unrelated to the outcomes the president seeks, the *way* they are used surely counts for a lot. If President Carter invested great time and energy into learning intricate details of policy endeavors, he was working hard to develop a resource of limited political utility. If President Reagan used his time guardedly, but invested it in persuading Congress about the merits of his policy, he enhanced the prospects of realizing his policy objectives even though time *per se* did not contribute independently to the outcome. Said House Minority Leader Robert H. Michel during President Reagan's successful 1982 tax hike campaign, "No president in my memory has been willing to devote so much time to individual members [of

Congress].''[55] During the successful budget campaign, ''Reagan used the time he had [a brief period to lobby Congress] to stunning effect.''[56] But President Carter, even in success, was less likely to spend his time the same way. During ratification of the Panama Canal treaties, ''some congressmen maintain[ed] that Carter [had] not courted members of the House and Senate energetically enough.''[57] For a president inclined to work hard, it was the wrong place for a lapsed effort.

SUMMARY

All thirty-four policy cases are characterized by fairly high levels of access between Congress and the White House. However, policy successes consistently demonstrate the highest levels of access, suggesting that extensive attention to access channels may enhance the president's prospects of attaining his objectives, possibly by making effective bargaining more possible.

This pattern holds specifically for access between Congress and the president. Data from the Carter and Reagan administrations indicate both chief executives were perceived as extremely accessible during instances of policy success. Carter administration personnel were also more accessible to Congress during policy success than policy failure; the Reagan staff was perceived to be highly accessible at all times. However, both staffs—as well as both presidents—carried on their most effective contacts with Congress during successful endeavors.

Three resources are not related to outcomes in systematic fashion, although two may contribute indirectly to presidential policy success. Charm and charisma do not appear to be related to the outcomes that Carter and Reagan attained. Data indicate that President Reagan was widely perceived to be the more charismatic of the two presidents, but this perception did not change during times when he did not achieve his policy objectives. Charm may be of secondary value to a president as a resource that promotes effective persuasion. Similarly, presidential effort applied to endeavors previously determined to be related to outcomes, such as effective persuasion or the development of an efficient organization, may bolster the president's chances for success. But, hard work in its own right is not related to the president's policy fortunes.

Technical expertise, or facility with information and detail, is also unrelated to success. President Carter was perceived to hold a greater command of detail than President Reagan, but his expertise was at its greatest during his failed initiatives. Likewise, Reagan was able to succeed without high evaluations of expertise. This suggests that Carter's tendency to invest effort and time into learning policy details was misguided.

SEVEN

Power and Context

> Ronald Reagan was relaxed. The pace was leisurely, the humor abundant. When the New Jersey Congressman sitting beside him on the Oval Office sofa Thursday afternoon expressed fears that workers being laid off in his district were too old to find new jobs, the President quipped: "What do you mean?—I got one at 70." . . . And so Representative Matthew J. Rinaldo, a moderate Republican from Union, NJ, who had gone to the White House to say he was concerned over the President's proposals to cut spending for mass transit, education, health and social services, emerged from the half-hour session with a pair of Presidential cufflinks. He had left his vote behind.[1]

Resources work together. When President Reagan emulsified the fears of Congressman Rinaldo, he used several resources that we have found to be related to results: personal access to the Oval Office, the small favor, gentle persuasion in the form of the humor-filled soft sell. This particular combination worked for Ronald Reagan in this circumstance with this particular congressman; another president might act differently, as might this president at another point in his term. In 1981, such presidential visits were still novel, and the Reagan touch was still overwhelming Washington. When the novelty wanes, effectiveness naturally follows.

As resources are used collectively, their relative impact is important. It would be useful for us to know of the extent to which, say, persuasion effects success relative to the impact of organization or access, even if the specific combinations vary from instance to instance. I will not consider anything so precise as a "formula" for outcomes, given the complexity of the matter and the ambiguity involved in measuring the resources of which I speak. But, consideration should be given to the use of resources in a collective sense. Analysis thus far indicates that bargaining as a form of persuasion, organizational efficiency, and White House access are related in a systematic fashion to policy outcomes. That is to say, these resources are observed to be used most frequently during successful policy initiatives across administrations. This is especially so for the Carter and Reagan administrations, despite their obvious differences in legislative agenda and political style. The relative importance of these "power" resources will be considered here.

Furthermore, presidential power is not exercised in a vacuum. External factors will have an impact upon the extent to which the president can utilize power resources, and how they will be received. Had the unemployment rate in Union, N.J., been 10 percentage points higher, Congressman Rinaldo might have been less responsive to the president's quip, no matter how well delivered, no matter how much personal access was being granted, no matter how dearly he may have coveted those cufflinks bearing the Official Seal. Thus far, context has been largely overlooked, except in the discussion of factors pertinent to organizational efficiency, which are beyond the president's control. The power variables discussed may well be related to outcomes, but their net importance is bound to be influenced by situational forces such as the state of the nation and existing levels of public support for the president.[2] This chapter will consider the place of power resources in the context in which they are exercised.

ANALYSIS

Numerous contextual factors could be assumed to influence the president's ability to exercise power. Initially, six items were considered for their theoretical importance and common-sense value.

1. *Congressional composition*. The composition or partisan breakdown of Congress during the period of each policy case was examined. At any time, the president's party might control both houses of Congress, as was the case during the entire Carter administration; the opposition party

might control both houses of Congress, as was the case during the entire Nixon and Ford presidencies; or control might be split, as it was during the first Reagan term.

2. *Gallup approval ratings*. Calculated almost monthly during the period under study, these provide an ongoing measure of public support for the job the president is doing, and as such, a good estimate of the president's "public prestige."[3]
3. *Economic factors*. The state and direction of the economy were estimated with two commonly used measures: mean monthly changes in the Consumer Price Index, and the average unemployment rate for the period of each policy case.
4. *Presidential honeymoons*. These may be assumed to be periods of bipartisan goodwill.[4] In these periods a new president is expected first to chart a course for government and, although more fictitious than factual, to make a fast impact.
5. *Vietnam War/Watergate Scandal*. Two of the largest social and political influences of the time period under study were examined for their effects on presidential productivity.[5]

Preliminary analysis made it possible to specify important contextual factors more precisely. The economic measures, the Vietnam war, and Watergate could be seen as "components" of public approval[6] and were determined to be items on which evaluations of presidential performance were based.[7] Because of their more specific nature, they were used in lieu of the Gallup ratings in assessing policy effects. The intensity of the Vietnam war and the presence of the Watergate scandal demonstrated a limited impact on presidential effectiveness, most likely because a sizable number of cases occurred either before or after these events. Because of this, neither is included in subsequent analysis; however, it is plausible and intuitive that both had an impact for a brief period when each crisis was at its height.

The "honeymoon period" also has no apparent impact on outcome, an observation consistent with the poor results attained by Carter during his first months and with the dearth of policy cases decided during the early days of any of the administrations studied. The impact of congressional composition, likewise, was limited and statistically insignificant. This, too, is consistent with the findings discussed previously: whereas congressional composition would remain fixed for periods of years, often for the duration of entire administrations, individual presidents would encounter both success and failure while in office.

The strongest contextual factors were the economic ones; these will be discussed along with the power variables that prior analysis suggests are consistently related to policy outcomes—organizational efficiency, access, and bargaining as a form of persuasion. The result is a model that incorporates both elements of power and elements of the environment in which power is wielded, in an effort to understand the relative influences of each on the results the president attains.[8]

Logistic regression was employed to assess the relative importance of power and contextual factors on the likelihood that the president would successfully achieve the policy outcomes he desired. *Policy success,* as defined in Chapter 1 and used throughout this book, constitutes the achievement of a large-scale domestic policy initiative that the president actively sought through the exercise of power. In the simple fashion employed here, *policy failure* is the opposite result, making the outcome we seek to explain dichotomous; that is, it may either occur or not occur. Logistic regression is appropriate for such situations where the dependent variable is dichotomous.[9]

The discussion that follows is meant to be exploratory. My objective is to clear the way for future discussion of what happens when presidents succeed, based on an initial understanding of what happened in the past when power met circumstance. Although the thirty-four cases observed is large relative to the universe of salient presidential domestic initiatives undertaken between 1964 and 1982, it is quite small in comparison to the sample sizes employed by others who have used similar analytical techniques.[10] And, of course, the scope of the subject is broad.

The model specified for testing includes three power and two contextual variables. I examine the probability of attaining a successful outcome as

$$Pr\,(\text{Success}) = \frac{1}{1 + \exp^{(-X\beta)}}$$

where $X\beta = \beta_0 + \beta_1 ACC_t + \beta_2 BAR_t + \beta_3 ORG_t + \beta_4 CPI_t + \beta_5 UNP_t + u_t$ and

β_0 = constant

ACC_t = access allowed to the executive branch

BAR_t = presidential bargaining

ORG_t = executive branch organizational efficiency

CPI_t = average monthly change in the consumer price index

UNP_t = average unemployment rate (percent)

u_t = error term

Results of the logit analysis may be found in Table 7.1. The model estimates the likelihood of attaining policy success, given the values of the exogenous variables.[11] As Table 7.2 indicates, it provides a strong basis for determining the success of policy initiatives, which are predicted correctly in 88 percent of the cases.[12] We can

Table 7.1. Logit Analysis of the Predictors of Presidential Policy Outcomes

Explanatory Variable	Estimated Coefficient	Standard Error	*t*-Statistic
Constant	−0.83	0.61	−1.364
Power Variables			
Access	5.27	2.44	2.162*
Bargaining	0.99	0.98	1.012
Organization	21.52	10.69	2.011*
Contextual Variables			
CPI	−5.19	2.65	1.959
Unemployment	−0.55	0.24	2.285*

*Significance < .05; G^2 = 19.52, Significance < .005.

Table 7.2. Accuracy of Logit Analysis Predictions of Policy Outcomes

	Actual Policy Outcomes	
Predicted Policy Outcomes	Failure	Success
Failure	13	0
Success	4	17

Percentage of correct predictions = 88; N = 34

infer four important things from the results: (1) organizational efficiency and the access hypothesized to follow from it are important predictors of policy outcome; (2) bargaining surprisingly is not an important predictor of results; (3) both power and context contribute to effectiveness; and (4) the state of the economy places a significant restraint on the president's ability to attain policy results that may be wholly unrelated to economic conditions.

Organization and Access

As preliminary analysis suggests, organizational efficiency and access to the White House are strong predictors of policy outcomes, suggesting a primary role for each in the causal structure of policy success. The coefficients associated with both are statistically significant (significance $< .05$) and large, although the large amount of variability associated with organization makes for an inefficient estimator. This is consistent with some of the extreme evaluations of efficiency—both high and low—recorded during the Nixon, Carter, and Reagan administrations.

As expected, the likelihood of success increases with greater efficiency and greater access. Organization, especially, has been described as a boundless quantity, in the sense that the president may continually improve the efficiency of his staff in the effort to obtain a smoother working relationship with Congress. We will see shortly that there appears to be a threshold efficiency level that varies with the state of other power and contextual forces, beyond which the chances for policy success improve dramatically. At this point, it is apparent that efficiency promotes success to a great extent.

Access is similarly related to outcomes, a quality that improves the president's chances the more it is available. This, too, is consistent with prior analysis. We would expect favorable results to be associated with open communication lines between the president, the president's staff, and Congress, much as the successful policy outcomes explored here were clearly characterized by conditions of openness and effective communication. In this respect, open access may be treated as a fundamental condition for policy success, much as we might treat organizational efficiency.

As anticipated, the two work together. Previously, I hinted at a causal structure, in which efficient executive organization encourages an effective relationship with Congress. Organization, in short, makes access possible, or at least more likely. This relationship is certainly not disputed here. It is quite possible that the elements of Ronald Reagan's deftly run White House made possible the ongoing dialogue with Congress that characterized his successful 1981 budget initiative. His experienced, well-regarded liaison staff, a high degree of consensus over goals, the recognition of the need to communicate with Congress, and the ability to communicate that need effectively among White House staffers all contributed to a White House in which access was an ongoing occurrence. Without internal communication it would have been harder for all parties to be involved; take away the experience of the chief legislative liaison operatives and access would have been more difficult to achieve.

Recall that the Carter White House suffered both poor organization and limited access to Congress in early 1977. Although a congressional dialogue was not a presidential priority, would it have been more likely had top liaison personnel been more experienced in the ways of Washington politics? Might relations with Congress have been more fluid had the White House itself been oriented more toward conflict resolution and presentation of collective goals? We do know that policy failure becomes more probable as both efficiency and access decline. The two appear to work together, to define the conditions under which the president and his staff approach Congress and the task at hand. Although clearly not the only determinates of outcome, among the things that can be controlled they go a long way toward demarcating the president's chances. Successful outcomes begin at home.

This understanding of access as a global characteristic of presidential effectiveness should be distinguished from the effects of access to the president by individual policy actors. I suggested at the start of this chapter that Congressman Rinaldo might have been less likely to move toward President Reagan's position had his visit to the Oval Office merely been one in a long string of similar occurrences. On the individual level, the carefully placed invitation can be an effective form of persuasion, which, if overworked, would be expected to lose its effectiveness. It is important to remember that access in this individual sense is not what is being considered here. Clearly available to the clever politician who seeks to enhance his bargaining power, access as a particular is primarily a tool of persuasion. Regular, open channels of communication with Congress, in turn, are vehicles from which *all* forms of persuasion may be exercised. Unlike the individual case, the value of such regular interaction will not dwindle or decrease.

Organizational efficiency has been treated here as a relative entity, as a condition best defined by the ratio of references of efficiency to inefficiency. Except in unusual circumstances, such as during Reagan's MX debacle, inefficient organizations will be credited with *some* degree of operating ability. This allows for an element of disarray in even the finest operations. But, at some juncture, minor difficulties accumulate to the point where they become the norm. How much inefficiency can the White House tolerate before it begins to affect the president's chances for success?

The logit equation may be interpreted in such a way as to determine the marginal impact of organizational efficiency on the likelihood of presidential policy success.[13] The figures to be discussed are illustrative and should be interpreted as hypothetical measures illuminating broad principles. For instance, consider the variables included in the equation as they pertain to the 1977 Carter energy initiative. Organization was poor, access was restricted, and bargaining with Congress was limited. Unemployment was averaging 7.0 percent, and consumer prices were climbing at a monthly increment of better than 0.5 percent. All in all, conditions for success were far less than ideal.

Under the circumstances, it is hardly surprising that things turned out as they did. Nine in ten references made about Carter's White House during the energy project mentioned some form of inefficiency, giving Carter's organization an efficiency rating of .10. With organizational woes so vast, with access limited, with persuasion blunted, and with economic conditions less than great, there was virtually no chance that the president's initiative would succeed.[14]

Even with a somewhat more efficient White House, Carter's chances would have remained the same. All other factors being equal, had only seven in ten observations of Carter's organization been references to disarray, the president's chances for success would have been only .08. In other words, a .20 improvement in the evaluation of his organization would have increased Carter's chances for success by only 8 percentage points, to a level where a fortuitous outcome remained highly unlikely. If disorganization is extreme, or great, and accompanying circumstances are not helpful, the chances for success are small.

Of course, in Carter's case, disorganization was reinforced by the minimal use of other power resources and by a somewhat slow economy. It is possible that had Carter been supremely organized, all things being equal, his chances for success would have greatly improved. There is a threshold level of organizational efficiency beyond which organization improves the president's odds even if other factors still work against him. The exact threshold will vary with the circumstances; it will take more to compensate for disastrous economic conditions, for instance, than to mitigate against the effects of a sluggish economy. But, once the threshold is reached, the president's chances for success improve dramatically.

Take the case we have been considering, with circumstances much as they were during the energy initiative. Table 7.3 displays some of the possibilities. As we said, with an organizational efficiency ratio of .10, as was the case in 1977, Carter's chances for success were nil. With an organizational rating of .30, his chances remained poor. But an improvement in this rating to only .35 (in which only three and one-half of every ten organizational references mention efficiency) translates into a 35 percent chance for success; the odds remain against Carter, but they are not as long.

With a slight improvement beyond this, Carter would have crossed the "organizational threshold." Had the efficiency/inefficiency ratio been four to six, the odds for success would have shot up to .77, all other conditions being equal. Under the circumstances, the majority of references to Carter's organization could have remained negative; wires could have remained crossed on occasion, liaison officials at times could have missed important

Table 7.3. Hypothetical Outcome Probabilities Given Various Values of Organizational Efficiency, Holding Other Variables Constant at 1977 Levels

Value of Organizational Efficiency	.10	.30	.35	.40
Probability of Success	.00	.08	.35	.77

congressional votes. But, enough of an organization would have been in place to make the chances of success better than three in four.

This is similar to what happened during the Panama Canal treaties effort (although the actual level of organizational efficiency proved to be higher). Recall that the Carter organization was greatly improved. Secret planning and scattered agendas that characterized the early months were replaced with a more centralized effort to win approval for the treaties. Still, the Carter White House had difficulty getting organized at times, especially around small but important logistical matters such as getting a White House automobile to the right corner at the right time in order to meet Senator Zorinsky. Had economic circumstances been similar to those in effect during the energy initiative (and, in fact, they were), had access and persuasion continued at comparable levels (in fact, they were better), Carter's chances for Senate approval of the treaty would have been favorable even with an organization that was still struggling at times to sort itself out.

In most instances, the nature of the president's organization will not actually hover around the threshold level. As the data presented in Chapter 5 indicate, there is a stark difference in the character of the president's organization between successes and failures, making the measure of efficiency less continuous than it would appear to be here. It is misleading to believe that a gradual improvement in the president's operation could translate into an increase in the level of efficiency from .35 to .40, thus radically altering the odds for success. As Chapter 5 indicates, the types of items included under the organizational umbrella are often personnel oriented, rooted in the operational structure of the White House, and slow to change. A more appropriate way to regard this illustration is to consider the great difference that changes in organizational efficiency *could* make, given consistency among other relevant factors.

Of course, if greater efficiency yields greater access, as I have argued, all things would not likely be equal. As efficiency improves, we would expect the likelihood for improved access between the White House and Congress to improve accordingly. More likely, the mechanism for more widespread communication would be in place, whether or not improvements actually occurred.[15] We will not expressly consider the interaction between organization and access.[16] Both, however, are related to the domestic policy outcomes the president is likely to achieve. They are fundamental to his chances for success in the legislative arena, as they shape the conditions under which the president will approach Congress.

Bargaining

Contrary to prior analysis and conventional wisdom, bargaining does not appear to be a predictor of policy outcomes. The coefficient is small and fails to meet the test of statistical significance. This is surprising; when examined independently, those aspects of bargaining central to the persuasive process appear to make a difference. Personal flexibility, rapport, and the use of favors are encountered more frequently and, in most instances, used more effectively during successful policy cases.

I have nonetheless chosen to leave bargaining in the equation on the strength of prior analysis and because of its theoretical importance to outcomes. Even with the important roles played by organization and access, these resources address only the environment in which power relations will be played out. It is hard to imagine distinguishing success from failure solely on the basis of situation. Once the White House is ready for battle, once strategy is consistent and clear, once the lines of communication are operating between both ends of Pennsylvania Avenue, the president still has to *do* something. Though he may try both to dominate and persuade, the former bears no consistent relationship to the ends he achieves. The actions that may differentiate success from failure are those bargaining behaviors that could sway members of Congress to his position. Thus, bargaining meets the test of substantive importance even as it falls short of statistical significance.

Bargaining, in this respect, comes close to Neustadt's persuasive process. Through the careful use of favors and through well-placed personal flexibility, the president can best exercise the "skill and will" that Neustadt claims is necessary over time to preserve his professional reputation in official Washington. But, careful use is a matter of political skill, choice, and even a bit of luck. Just as Neustadt was unable to specify exactly how a president could protect his reputation, it is impossible to say which elements of bargaining should be used at any specific time. And, once a president has altered his position on a matter or offered a favor, he is hard-pressed to reverse himself without running the risk of giving the impression that flexibility is actually indecision.

This is the nature of bargaining. Its unpredictable characteristics may hold a clue as to why statistical analysis fails to indicate its substantive importance. Given the small coefficient associated with bargaining, should we attempt to estimate changes in the likelihood of success given a unit change in bargaining, we would find negligible differences. Although increased bargaining would predict a greater likelihood of success, as we would expect, the improvement would be small.

This is consistent with the way actual bargaining often progresses. To bargain is to attempt to move others toward your position by compromising with them, persuading them with favors or promises, or by establishing a rapport with them that generates a feeling of mutual interest. The process may have an influence on the other party, but that alone will not guarantee results. The actual outcome will depend more on the outcome of bargaining. We have already established that presidential bargaining effectiveness is greatest when presidents succeed. But, the reasons for such effectiveness lie beyond the simple use of the resources of bargaining, which are necessary to the president's objectives but not sufficient.

Resources of bargaining are finite. They may be overutilized and lose their effectiveness. We would not expect more bargaining to yield favorable results, nor would we expect to be able to predict outcomes simply on the basis of how extensively the resources of bargaining were engaged, no matter how important they may be to the final result. Some bargaining sessions are long and complex and lead nowhere; some efforts at persuasion result in stalemate. In 1982, President Reagan did not help matters by refusing for weeks to become involved in bipartisan negotiations with the congressional leadership over a tax increase. But, when he finally got personally involved, the result was little better, as "an extraordinary face-to-face bargaining session between President Reagan and House Speaker Thomas P. (Tip) O'Neill, Jr." ultimately "collapsed" without resolution.[17]

It follows that we may not be able to predict an improvement in the odds of success based simply on the use of resources designed to persuade. Unlike organizational efficiency, which once in place can continue to yield benefits save for the risks of deterioration brought on by staff attrition; unlike personal and staff access with Congress, which once in place could continue indefinitely to provide a channel for discourse; unlike these resources, bargaining and persuasion are finite. The president may continue to try to persuade long after the resources he brings to the effort have lost their effectiveness. He may continue to make phone calls, hold meetings with senators, even parcel out tie clips, but the effectiveness of the effort is not linear. It is not always the case that two favors can buy what one could not, and too much compromise could be seen as indecision.

Consider the different reactions generated by two presidents to largely the same bargaining behavior. In 1981, during the budget campaign, President Reagan involved himself in what was widely considered to be "horse-trading" for votes,[18] or "old-fashioned wheeling and dealing."[19] "In dozens of meetings with wavering Congressmen over recent days, Mr. Reagan has persistently asked the question: 'What can I do to help you make up your mind?' "[20] The answers were quick to come. At several points during the spring and summer of that year, the president was able to bargain and persuade his way to more votes for his version of the budget. Each presidential blitz "took its toll" as Reagan "nailed down" the support of wavering lawmakers while the congressional opposition "conceded there is little the Democrats can do to outbid the president in the favors game."[21]

Three years earlier, an equally intensive effort by President Carter met with less emphatic results from members of Congress of his own party. "Carter's own lobbying efforts far exceeded anything that he had previously attempted. He met or spoke with all hundred senators at least once over the past couple of months, and made eighty-seven phone calls in the last two weeks alone. Some fence-sitters . . . heard from him a half-dozen times."[22] The reason was to win support for the Panama Canal treaties, an objective the president ultimately attained. But his persuasive efforts met with mixed reactions. Whereas some senators were eventually moved by the Carter effort, others became more critical as the president turned up the heat. Senator Packwood said he was "disgusted" by some of the deals Carter was making, and at one point threatened to withdraw his support for the treaties because of it.[23] Even Senate Majority Leader Byrd was quoted as saying to aides that the president lost several votes because of heavy-handed tactics and "embarrassing suggestions of political deals."[24]

Carter was no less heavy handed in his bargaining than was Reagan. Yet to some, Carter's efforts were blatant and embarrassing, whereas Reagan's labors were simply effective. In the end, both presidents reached their policy objectives. But the extent to which each benefited from bargaining differed. Reagan's persuasive endeavors likely increased his chances of success in linear fashion; the more he bargained, the more he changed minds. Carter's efforts leveled off more sharply; although he continued to change some minds, he started losing support as his efforts drew to a conclusion before the Senate vote. The effect was closer to what we find here when we try to understand the relationship between bargaining and policy success.

From what we know about policy outcomes, different presidents using different formulas, for lack of a better word, have been more effective with their resources of persuasion during periods of success. One likely reason is increased organizational efficiency and greater access to Congress, making the resources of persuasion more consistently and clearly communicated, increasing the president's bargaining power. But it is hard to imagine the president successfully changing minds without engaging in effective bargaining, bringing to bear whatever political and interpersonal skills he brought with him to Washington.

Power and Context

From the previous discussion of organization and access, it should be apparent that both power variables and contextual factors contribute to the probability that the president will be successful. Economic conditions are foremost among contextual factors affecting the president's chances. Two estimates of economic conditions were included in the logit equation: average monthly changes in consumer prices and the mean unemployment rate for the duration of each policy case. Each appears to have an impact on policy results. Unemployment meets the standards of statistical significance at .05; consumer prices just barely miss the cut-off for statistical significance at the same level.

The power variables all have a positive impact on policy outcomes. That is, increases in organizational efficiency, access to Congress, and bargaining behavior are associated with an increase in the likelihood of success. The contextual variables, on the other hand, are negatively related to outcomes. This is to be expected: increases in consumer prices and high unemployment are associated with a decreased likelihood of presidential achievement. Note that the signs associated with the CPI and unemployment variables are negative, signifying that the chances for a propitious outcome decline as prices rise and as more people find themselves out of work.

This indicates that economic conditions constrain the president. Regardless of the substance of the particular case with which he is involved, the larger domestic situation as captured by the state and direction of the economy will have an effect on his ability to maneuver Congress. Earlier, it was suggested that economic factors are a strong predictor of presidential popularity. This appears to be an important link in the relationship between economic conditions and specific domestic policy outcomes.

Presidential popularity is a good approximation of the president's public prestige, his standing among Americans. The Gallup Poll asks simply for approval, whether or not individuals support the job the president is doing. The greater the support, the more the president will appear to be held in high esteem beyond the Beltway — a factor of no little significance inside the Capitol. To the extent that approval rises and falls with the economy, consumer prices and the unemployment picture provide a good approximation of how the president is doing. Although the association between economic conditions and support for the president is by no means absolute, it is persistent and strong. In the matter of policy success, we see how the economic picture can serve as a constraint on the likelihood that the president will accomplish major domestic objectives.

Had the policy cases included in this study been limited to the period of the late 1960s and early 1970s, it is quite possible that the intensity of domestic unrest caused by the Vietnam war and the Watergate scandal would have revealed the same constraining effects on the president. With the Vietnam war at its height, Lyndon Johnson avoided certain political punishment by refusing to run for a second full term; with the Watergate investigation closing in on the Oval Office, Richard Nixon chose resignation over impeachment. Under these circumstances, it is reasonable to believe that a tremendous constraint was placed on the likelihood for progress of whatever was left of either president's domestic agenda, assuming any energy could be directed away from the main difficulty at hand.

The economic variables employed here, then, act to approximate the impact of salient domestic concerns on the president's domestic policy performance. Economic conditions are merely the most consistent of these, at times, but not always the most prominent. However, we can learn of their impact on policy outcomes by examining the particular constraining effects of consumer prices and unemployment. The context in which the president operates will not seal his fate one way or the other; it will neither assure success nor make it unattainable. But it will constrain or enhance his power as it influences the way he is received by the nation, raising or lowering his baseline chances for success. What he does within this setting remains a function of how he exercises power: how he operates the White House, communicates with Congress, and bargains.

Economic Factors

A useful way to understand how the economy constrains presidential performance is to consider the marginal effect of economic factors on the likelihood of success. This may be done similarly to the evaluation of the marginal effect of unit increases in organizational efficiency on the probability of success, by determining appropriate, hypothetical values for each exogenous variable and altering only the value associated with organizational efficiency. Consider two hypothetical situations: one, in which the president is in tenuous control of essential power variables; the other, in which he wields power with moderate effectiveness.[25] In each case, we will consider how the likelihood of achieving a successful outcome is influenced by changes in the average monthly rate of increase in consumer prices.

The first situation is analogous to Jimmy Carter's situation in 1977. At the time, the president's organization was in disarray. James Schlesinger was developing large pieces of the energy program in relative secrecy; Frank Moore was learning on the job how to handle the demands of legislative liaison, often leaving phone calls unreturned and messages unanswered; a group of relatively inexperienced top advisors was struggling unsuccessfully with developing and instituting a strategy for the energy program. Members of Congress reported widespread resistance by the White House to opening a dialogue with either the president or his surrogates. For his part, President Carter was reluctant to persuade the legislature to go along with his energy plans. His posture toward Congress was perceived to be rigid and unbending, and he was loathe to engage in persuasive maneuvers in an effort to win supporters.

In short, the president was not making use of his power resources, or he was not using them effectively. Under these circumstances, the context in which he operates means very little. Assuming poor organization, limited access, curtailed bargaining behavior, and a moderate to high unemployment rate, consumer prices have virtually no effect on the president's chances for success. Regardless of economic conditions, the chances for a favorable outcome are slim.

If consumer prices during this period were rising at a modest average monthly rate of 0.2 percent, the likelihood of a successful outcome would nonetheless be slimmer than one chance in ten. Were consumer prices to rise faster, the president's chances would diminish even further, but there is admittedly not very far for them to go. Table 7.4 tells the story more precisely. A rise in the average

Table 7.4. Hypothetical Outcome Probabilities Given Various Values of Average Monthly Change in CPI, for Two Hypothetical Scenarios

Assuming Poor Use of Power Resources				
Value of Average Monthly Change in CPI	.20	.30	.40	.50
Probability of Success	.09	.04	.02	.02
Assuming Moderately Effective Use of Power Resources				
Value of Average Monthly Change in CPI	.20	.30	.40	.50
Probability of Success	.91	.82	.65	.43

monthly increase in consumer prices from .20 to .30 lowers the probability of success 5 percentage points, from .09 to .04. A further increase in consumer prices to a monthly average of 0.4 percent lowers the president's chances a bit further, to a negligible .02. Should consumer prices rise to an average monthly rate of .50, the likelihood of policy success remains unaffected. In this instance, the president's proposal would be in such bad shape that a worsening economic situation would have no impact.

This may well be a worst-case scenario, in which the president works against his own cause through the misuse of the resources at his disposal. In an instance like this, he will find that good economic conditions will not give his policy a boost, and that unfavorable economic circumstances cannot rightly be blamed for his inability to succeed. Context matters much less than behavior. In an extreme situation such as this, the president would have failed to exercise those resources available to him which are most directly implicated in the causal structure of domestic policy success, and the reason for the long odds he would face could be directly attributed to his actions.

Given a less extreme scenario, context becomes more critical. Consider a hypothetical situation in which the president is more adept at using his power resources. Assume the White House is better organized, and the president is achieving a modest degree of success communicating with Congress, a situation analogous to the Panama Canal treaties ratification drive or the Carter natural gas compromise. Further, assume that the president is utilizing some of his bargaining tools and doing so with a degree of effectiveness. All told, one could assume that the president was in good shape on the basis of his use of key power resources.

In a situation such as this one, if the economy were cooperating his probability for success would indeed be quite high. With an average monthly increase in consumer prices of 0.2 percent, the president's chances for success would be better than nine in ten; with an average increase of 0.3 percent, better than eight in ten. Even if consumer prices were increasing by 0.4 percent monthly, the president's odds would be far better than chance.

But, if prices were to rise more sharply, the context in which the president operates would begin to take its toll. An average monthly increase in the CPI of .50 would make the likelihood of success .43, lowering the president's odds below the chance level and making them substantially less than they would be if, all things being equal, the economy was more cooperative. While a probability of success of .43 is far from a longshot, the effect of circumstance can be felt. In real terms, the difference is the resistance the president would feel in Washington over the impact of higher prices as it translates into more limited public support for his performance. As his public image suffers, his power resources become that much less effective, as members of Congress are ever aware of the overlap between their constituents and the president's constituents.

This in no way means that the president would not be successful in a situation where he was exercising key power resources effectively while consumer prices were rising steadily. It simply means that he would have to work harder against longer odds. Circumstances, in this sense, delimit the baseline likelihood that the president will succeed; obviously, the more favorable the domestic climate, the better the president's odds. But, as with the first example, ultimately the president's actions determine whether the odds will be bested. Even in the most favorable circumstance, in which a good economic climate reinforces effective behavior, the result is simply the strong probability of a favorable outcome.

In most of the cases studied, economic factors had no direct relationship to the substance of the policy proposal. Rather, the impact of the economy was felt through the effect it had on the president's overall public approval. A president riding high on the crest of a growing economy, such as Lyndon Johnson in his early days as president, operates in an environment conducive to the effective use of power resources. But, those resources must still be employed skillfully. Contextual factors simply provide a baseline from which to operate, making success more or less likely but leaving the ultimate judgment to the actions the president takes.

Skillful use of power resources can even mitigate against the negative effects of context. In 1981, when Ronald Reagan ushered in his "revolution" by reversing federal spending priorities, economic conditions were not the rosiest. Over the course of his budget effort, unemployment averaged 7.3 percent and consumer prices were rising at a monthly average of almost 0.8 percent—better than 0.2 percentage points higher than the rate President Carter experienced four years earlier. Yet, an outstanding organization, excellent communication, and persuasive bargaining skills combined for a successful outcome nonetheless. Just as contextual factors alone cannot assure success, neither can a mixed or unhappy economic picture be seen as a reliable predictor of ultimate failure. More accurately, the context in which the president operates provides a useful baseline for determining how effective he must be with his power resources in order to accomplish his objectives. From there, success becomes more likely with the skillful exercise of appropriate power resources.

CONCLUSIONS

As a first, sketchy picture of the characteristics of successful domestic policy outcomes emerges from the data, it becomes apparent that policy success is the product of several influences combining in any number of ways. Far from being defined by rigid parameters, success appears to be a function of contextual factors beyond the president's control and power resources in his grasp, working together in one of many possible combinations.

If domestic circumstances are favorable, the president may find that his resources take him further, that he need not be as attentive to communicating with Congress, for Congress will find it most important to communicate with him. If conditions are less favorable, he will likely have to work harder, or take more care, making sure to maximize those things more directly manipulable than the economy, such as organizational efficiency and bargaining ability.

But, just as there are different possible combinations of factors that could lead to success, so are there several resources that have a strong bearing on outcomes and, as such, should be maximized by any president hoping to enact a domestic agenda. Recent successful efforts have been characterized by an efficiently run White House and open lines of access with Congress, as well as the effective use of bargaining resources central to the persuasive process. Regardless of what other resources the president has at his disposal, these are the items that should command the most presidential attention. Each contributes in its own way to the likelihood of a favorable outcome, and each, to a certain extent, is under the president's control.

This means that the president needs to prepare before he can persuade. To the extent that he hopes to use his power to enact important domestic legislation, he needs to be organized and open as much as he needs to know how to bargain. No matter how skillful he may be in the ways of interpersonal dialogue, no matter how compelling a presence, if he hopes to move sufficient numbers of other policy actors to support his position, the president first needs to establish the apparatus to support the effort. The art of bargaining may close the deal, but to maximize his chances for success the president should look beyond persuasion, to the condition of the White House staff and his relationship with Congress.

The variables examined here are necessarily broad; as such, the conclusions we can draw are preliminary. But they suggest several specific places to look to further our understanding of the mechanics of presidential power. In particular, the several elements of organizational efficiency discussed in Chapter 5 may be examined in greater detail to assess the independent impact of each on policy outcomes and to determine more specific links to the persuasive process. Other contextual factors besides the economic considerations addressed here could be considered for the role they play in constraining the president's chances for success. And power may be addressed in other contexts beyond the narrow scope described earlier. It is quite reasonable that different or additional factors come into play when power is exercised in the foreign policy arena or for the purpose of domestic political gain. Given different objectives, it is quite possible that different means apply, just as we find that the means to the same objective need adjustment in the face of contextual variation.

At the same time, we can begin to develop a sense of which resources play a prominent role and how they may work together. It follows that operational efficiency could enhance access, just as it follows that efficiency and access may provide a basis for increased bargaining effectiveness. Furthermore, it follows that the president's standing in the public will influence the way he is perceived by the political community in which he works, so that domestic circumstances will alter just how carefully and completely he needs to operate. To exercise power effectively is to understand the circumstances and to know where to focus attention, as much as it is to have the skills to organize, communicate, and persuade.

☆ ☆ ☆ ☆ ☆ ☆ ☆ ☆

Logistic regression is employed to assess the relative impact of power variables and contextual factors on the likelihood that the president will achieve his domestic policy goals. This approach is intended as an initial attempt to understand the relative contribution of power resources to outcomes and to place the exercise of power in a political context.

Select power variables and the domestic political situation, as measured by economic conditions, both affect the odds for success, although individual influences vary depending upon the particular combination of factors in evidence. Organizational efficiency continues to emerge as an important component of the conditions in effect when success is most likely. Access between the White House and Congress is also a strong and significant predictor of success, lending support to the hypothesis that communication between the branches is facilitated by an efficient organization. Bargaining behavior, such as flexibility and the use of favors, fails the test of statistical significance but is retained in the model because of the theroretical and substantive importance of persuasion, as supported by previous analysis. It is both reasonable and likely that effective bargaining behavior influences policy outcomes, although escalation of the simple act of bargaining does not.

Improving the White House organization can have a dramatic effect on the president's chances of realizing domestic objectives. But, organization per se is addressed as a quality that does not lend itself to incremental change, making it erroneous to believe that small improvements in staffing, coordination, internal communication, and the like could yield great differences in the president's actual chances.

As consumer prices and unemployment rise, the likelihood of success decreases, even if the policy under consideration is not related to economic conditions. Economic conditions serve as a shorthand measure of the president's popular support, which would be expected to decline with the economy. Events with significant domestic impact such as the Vietnam war and the Watergate scandal are hypothesized to act accordingly, although they are excluded from analysis because they occurred during only a portion of the period under study. Contextual factors constrain the president and will affect his ability to utilize his power resources, although the effect will vary depending on the status of the president's power resources.

EIGHT

Possibilities for Power

In the scheme of things, power is difficult to exercise from the Oval Office. Presidents, of course, manage to get things done, but the wonder is that they can accomplish as much as they do given all that works against them. The context in which they operate may not predetermine outcomes, but a weak economy (not an unfamiliar sight to recent chief executives) will constrain their effectiveness. They can bolster their position with the careful construction of an efficiently organized executive branch, staffed with capable individuals, complete with well-drawn lines of communication, built around effective procedures for conflict resolution. But presidents rarely interact on a regular basis with more than their most senior appointees, leaving them little margin for determining capability and even less opportunity to build the executive organization to their specifications. They can try to dominate Congress and bulldoze their way to accomplishment, but by constitutional design they lack the vantage point necessary to threaten or impose sanctions with regular effectiveness. If they are clever enough to build an effective organization and capable through that organization of maintaining open lines of communication with Congress, they can attempt to persuade through the very effective bargaining resources they inherit with the office. But this requires skill, the political acumen to recognize which resources to use and when to use them, and the ability to use them persuasively.

On this score, Neustadt was quite correct that personal proclivities promote power in presidents. But the force of personality alone will not guarantee results, and it is a complex exercise to identify exactly *how* a president needs to act in order to maximize his chances for success at a given time, no less to determine what items he needs to bring to the effort. For that matter, it is always easier to identify what works and what doesn't than it is to suggest how to effect what matters. This is not a new problem; it was one thing for Neustadt to identify the importance of such things as professional reputation to remaining persuasive in Washington, but it was much harder (perhaps impossible) to identify exactly how to protect it.

For my part, I don't intend to suggest that I can identify how a president may utilize his resources so that power may persist and endure. Such would be pretentious even for a project that did not bill itself as preliminary. Still, I believe it is possible to identify four factors pertaining to power that derive from the findings presented here which may help determine the extent to which presidents are likely to utilize their resources in the manner this work indicates may lead to propitious outcomes. They are, in no particular order, understanding what's important, the president's psychological orientation, the context or environment in which the president operates, and institutional factors relating to the complexity of the executive branch. Some of these are within the president's reach to control or develop; others are entirely beyond his grasp.

FACTORS PERTAINING TO POWER

Understanding What Is Important

Given the wealth of resources available for a president to use, it appears a complex matter to distinguish the useful from the extraneous, especially when at face value everything seems potentially important. On this count, the evidence is clear that such apparently helpful resources as charm, expertise, and initiative were not systematically useful to contemporary presidents in their domestic policy campaigns. So, although the issue of what to employ and what to overlook may appear complex, this is one area where empirical research can go a long way to clarify the picture. Investing great sums of energy in learning the minute details of policy will not enhance the policy's legislative prospects, a lesson Jimmy Carter was late to learn. Possessing the charm of a favorite uncle may work some of the time, but it shouldn't be depended upon. If anything, the utility of energy lies less in exhibiting it than in focusing it on areas that have proven effective for past presidents in previous campaigns. Thus, energy spent on developing the organization of the White House is useful, not for its own sake, but for the investment made in developing efficiency.

More subtle but equally important is the ability to make political calculations that will maximize the effectiveness of the resources that *can* help the president. For instance, personal flexibility is positively associated with policy achievements; contemporary presidents have tended to be more flexible when they have succeeded. Knowing this should enable the president to take stock of the positions he takes on items of importance to him. But being flexible involves more than this; it entails knowing when something matters enough that a flexible posture is warranted. And it necessitates sufficient political judgment to determine accurately how those actions are received.

Flexibility, after all, exists only in relation to inflexibility, and can benefit the president only to the extent that those with whom he seeks to compromise view the behavior as something of value. To be flexible all the time means risking being seen as uncommitted or wishy-washy and ultimately less persuasive when it matters. In the end, judgments about flexibility, as with all resources, are made by others, and the fine line between gracious adaptability and wimpishness rests with the way behavior is interpreted. This applies to moments over the course of a campaign, when flexibility late to develop can stand in sharp contrast to previous stubbornness and help the president's cause. Remember that even during policy successes there were moments when the presidents studied here were inflexible or did not budge, and it is quite possible that they eventually benefited from perceived changes in their behavior as much as from the flexible postures they eventually assumed. It also applies to making choices between campaigns, ranking policy objectives and giving ground only when success is the highest priority in order to guard against being perceived as soft or malleable.

The difference between the rather straightforward effort to designate flexibility as a useful resource and the more subtle endeavor to use it well, in keeping with a theme developed previously, is the difference between the science of power and the art of its use. To know instinctively when to give ground and when to stand firm or, for that matter, simply to know how to make maximal use of important power resources—these are the domain of the politician, not the political scientist. For this reason, we can go only so far in delineating the outlines of presidential power. Thus, I end this section at the opposite pole from which it began, with a thought on how limited the empirical study of power may be. More on this shortly.

Psychological Factors

No matter what we may be able to tell the president about how to maximize his power resources, there may be things he simply is unable to do. Unlike recognizing what resources are important, we would expect that in some cases things that appear to benefit the president's cause are beyond his psychic makeup to employ. We cannot, for example, expect a president to give ground on an item of great personal importance, no matter how strongly the data indicate this to be his most politically expedient course of action. As one member of the Reagan White House said of the former president's feelings about tax increases, his objection was so "deep in his gut" that flexibility on the matter was for a long time simply not a consideration. Jimmy Carter's initial feelings about pork-barrel politics were much the same, keeping him from trading favors with a Democratic Congress excited about regaining the perks of the executive branch, hurting his energy program in the process.

Such attitudes may easily be misinterpreted as the lack of political skill, but in fact they go deeper. Often issue specific (Reagan was quite flexible about nontax matters), they speak to the psychological makeup of the person in office. Any president is susceptible to experiencing some personal resistance to the use of one or more of the resources that could help him achieve his ends. Access to others, for instance, requires a person who feels comfortable working with people on a regular basis. Someone who is fearful of such connections, like Richard Nixon, or someone who is guarded about who he lets in is likely to have some trouble with this, although the magnitude of difficulty clearly will be greatest in the former case. Regardless of how much it may benefit him politically, the psychological inclination must exist if the resource is to be employed. It is not a simple matter of recognizing what works and then doing it.

In this respect, presidential personality enters prominently into the power picture. But, it does so in a manner that I believe to be quite different from the primary treatment it enjoys in the traditional literature. Personality in this sense is a factor that may intervene in the effective use of resources that themselves may be entirely unrelated to the person of the president. It affects the way resources are used or, once again, the art of power. If the president's inclination is to neglect the operation of the White House for whatever reason (and this could be ignorance of its importance as easily as it could be the consequence of a psychological predisposition), personality factors may function as an important contributing cause of why the president did not maximize his power. If he simply is the sort that cannot organize, the problem lies in the makeup of the person, with obvious consequences for his organization.

Conversely, personal proclivities can enhance the use of other resources. No doubt when Ronald Reagan offered a presidential favor, the "aw shucks" smile for which he was famous had an endearing effect on the way in which it was received. Jimmy Carter, never the game-show host, was ill received even when he tried to use favors as a resource. In this sense, whereas the independent effects of charm or charisma were negligible, their impact on the use of an important, nonpersonal resource may have been prodigious. The role of personality is again great, again secondary. The resource of import is the favor, which is entirely unrelated to the personality of the individual offering it. Personality simply may enhance the effectiveness of the delivery system.

There is no way for a person to learn to be a slick master of ceremonies, just as it is impossible for a naturally rigid individual to become genuinely flexible or for someone innately disorganized to change in office. The psychology of the person is largely fixed when he becomes president and, all promises for growth in office aside, will influence the way he manages the resources of his office that themselves are entirely unrelated to character or personality. The fact that the office responds to the individual remains an inevitability in the exercise of presidential power, but one that I believe matters most for the implications it has with respect to the way several clearly identifiable and nonpersonal resources may or may not be employed.

Environmental Factors

Much like the psychological variables, the context in which the president works is largely beyond his control, although here social or political rather than psychic distance defies the president's grasp. The model discussed in Chapter 7 includes a central role for the influence of economic conditions on the president's power chances. If inflation and unemployment are down, the prospects for domestic policy success are up. Also addressed briefly but excluded from formal consideration are large-scale political or social factors, such as the Vietnam war and the Watergate scandal, whose effect over time was marginal but which it is reasonable to believe would have to have an impact on presidential effectiveness at their stormy peak.

Such are the macroevents with which a president must deal. But, as success itself is a variable quantity that changes within as well as between administrations, those that may fluctuate over brief periods, like economic health, appear to make the most marked impact. These would be analogous to the political cycles and trends of which Rockman speaks, which may complete a full revolution over a narrow period of time. When Jimmy Carter was inaugurated, Congress was in the throes of an assertive phase in its approach to the White House, and public political pressure called for a restrained chief executive. Within two years, the yearning for a strong president had returned, and within four, Congress had assumed a more passive posture.

Some of what a president must deal with is inherited; Carter was the product of a time that demanded a truncated president, but then he had to live with those demands while in office. Some of the president's context may be attributed to his own actions, as is asserted by those who argue that the advent of the call for a strong chief executive was hastened by Carter's early string of policy flubs. Economic circumstance, the macroevent that specifically has been linked to presidential policy outcomes, may be seen in this light. At the onset, the president inherits a set of economic conditions; eventually, they become attributed to what he did (or did not do) during his term. The state of OPEC and the size of the deficit aside, this may be a reasonable attribution to make, and the president can to some extent enhance his prospects with noneconomic domestic matters by achieving success with programs designed to control inflation and keep people on the job. Of course, this kind of success need be measured not in the simple shorthand of getting legislation through Congress, but by the impact the program has on the economy, a matter far more complex than identifying important resources and using them effectively.

If there is a place where the president can directly influence the context in which he wields power, it is among items of his own choosing. Beyond the demands of the time in which he serves, a president approaches his agenda in a manner of his own choosing. Some times call for specific or immediate action, but it is still the president's prerogative to determine the shape of the response. Johnson was adept at managing a large domestic policy wish list, where Carter was not. Reagan introduced significant changes in America's approach to social spending without introducing a lot of legislation. The number of items on the agenda matters less than the president's ability to handle them. Ronald Reagan probably could not have handled Johnson's full platter, and in fact with his advisors made a deliberate choice to focus strictly on the budget in 1981. Although Carter needed to address the energy issue, he didn't have to introduce and then adhere to the massive program that became known as his would-be energy plan. Perhaps personal misbelief or a misreading of Washington politics led him to both take on the unchewable mouthful and then not recognize that the food was clogging his air passages. Either way, he acted against his cause by unnecessarily sullying the context in which he worked. The resulting wound was all the more hurtful given the limited maneuvering room provided the president by his environment.

Institutional Factors

In a very real sense, it is unlikely for one person to be able to coordinate any organization as large as the institutional presidency. The challenge is simply too great: for one person to exercise enough control over so many individuals with their own minds and interests. This is borne out by the fact that no president—not even those who temporarily mastered the secrets of the executive branch—was perceived to maintain an "efficient" organization at all times. The best laid plans are subject to the public sector's revolving door, to unexpected internal division over policy, to accidental misunderstanding leading to temporary breakdown in communication, to "good hires" turning out unexpectedly wrong.

At the very least, the president may be able to be aware of the elements of organizational efficiency that factor in to the outcomes he is likely to achieve. This may also be the very most he can do. As the intended disjuncture among institutions mandates cooperation by design, the unforseen growth in and commensurate complexity of the institutional presidency adds an unintended degree of organizational horror to the president's job. Not only need he concern himself with the ability to persuade effectively those with a different institutional vantage point and different political responsibilities, he must reign in a cumbersome White House organization to maximize his ability to do so. And the effective exercise of power by one person becomes dependent on the behavior of the many who act in his name.

IS POWER POSSIBLE?

All this makes it seem as if presidential power is an unlikely objective. It may be. Certainly, the system mitigates against it by virtue of its size, by constitutional design, and by necessitating that so many things fall into place for objectives to be attained. It is unlikely, perhaps, but it is not impossible. Given the complexity of the system, it is impressive that presidents at times do achieve their ends, sometimes stunningly smoothly, sometimes after painstaking toil. But they do succeed. Even those presidents remembered as hapless by history had their triumphs. And although triumphant presidents may be remembered as invincible, the truth is that they, too, had their moments of defeat. Only in legend could a president retire from office with an unblemished policy record.

Of course, some presidents succeed more often than others, or effect more globally important results, although such counting and ranking may be dangerously influenced by historical value judgments and, worse, threatens to change the point. Ronald Reagan's failure to win support for the MX missile with the Dense Pack basing scheme had widespread implications for the defense industry and national defense policy. Jimmy Carter's failure to win support for the energy program was critical to multiple policy communities and to the direction of American energy policy. Can we equate one loss with the other? In policy terms the answer is no, because the oranges differ too greatly from the apples. But in political terms, where political fruit are similar, we probably can say that Carter was hurt more because the defeat was protracted and came at the start of his term, unlike Reagan's MX debacle, which occurred, short and sweet, during a lame duck season of Congress in his second year.

Still, the assessment of the damage is political, even though the objective of the endeavor was policy. With few exceptions, this is how we tend to remember our presidents, by how they fared when doing what they did, perhaps more than by what they actually accomplished. This is consistent with the way Neustadt viewed power, as something of an end as well as a means to that end, and I believe it is a trap into which we are all prone to fall, layperson and expert alike.

If we focus instead on policy, on the results of the game rather than the game itself, we will still find some presidents with more "victories" than others. But we may also capture a simple but often overlooked point: accomplishments are within the grasp of all presidents, regardless of how complicated the system may be, no matter how much the playing rules may be stacked against it. Policy triumphs are at once remarkable and commonplace: remarkable, because of the complexity of the levers on the power machinery; commonplace, because a working combination is so regularly uncovered. Given a system that, on scrutiny, makes presidential accomplishment seem extraordinary, the consistency of successful results if not their number make for eye-opening interest.

Power is possible because certain resource combinations will work for the president, and because *these* are relatively easy to identify. Whereas only political skill will convert them effectively, they are no less recognizable on investigation. Some presidents may stumble onto a working combination, others may methodically zero in, perhaps to find to their dismay that they cannot run the White House as they hoped they could or that the persuasive ability of favors has a limited life. But the combination is there, at least some of the time. Discovery can take a president partway to his objectives; this is the science of power. The rest of the journey requires skillful implementation, and the gentle marriage of science and art.

IS POWER DESIRABLE?

With the exception of the Ford-Carter years, the postwar presidency has been a strong one and, barring Eisenhower and perhaps Bush, an active one. Public expectations of great things have echoed in and been heightened by campaign rhetoric. Scholars who are wont to rank the presidents tend also to fall prey to the model of presidential strength. Only in the immediate post-Vietnam war, post-Watergate scandal world did we sing the praises of a limited presidency; and then before the echo from the chorus had dimmed in our ears the celebration of Reagan began. Once again, Americans want their presidents to fill the vast oceans in advance of walking on the water.

But, again, these desires tend to be more political than policy oriented, for they ask the president to assume a state of power, to *be* powerful, rather than to *do* anything in particular with it. Ronald Reagan did both, but the bulk of his major policy achievements came during his first year, in advance of seven years of "presiding." If power is measured by what the president does instead of how he reigns while doing it, then it is desirable to have, but within limits that fit nicely with what this work says about the likelihood that a president will achieve his ends.

I am suggesting that the president as advocate has a long road to follow, but that he can lighten his load by paying attention to the particulars of the resources he inherits when he takes the oath. To the extent that he can organize the White House effectively, and use this organization to maintain open channels with Congress, and use these channels to persuade—to the extent that he has the capability to do these things and do them effectively, he can maximize his prospects for success in a system carefully designed to frustrate individual initiative. As the only nationally elected office holder in the system, successful advocacy has its obvious benefits, and power, by extension, becomes a desirable attribute.

But it is equally so that the system is designed to frustrate for a reason, that too much successful advocacy of a particular position (no matter how much we may personally agree with it) has its dangers, that it is good that presidential power is complex enough to mitigate against indefinite policy winning streaks. Even the most masterful politician is not enough of a scientist and artist always to overcome the various psychological, environmental, and institutional constraints to power that are bound to face him along the way.

This is a healthy thing, considering what the opposite situation would mean for policy, to say nothing of the effects of power qua power on the person who would so regularly impose his way. The resulting muddle is a comfortable fate for us all. As design would have it, while there are constants to the exercise of power in the contemporary presidency, these require immense planning and a collective effort, not the sorts of things likely to enable one person to dominate. But, power is also more than persuasion or constitutionally derived powers, and it is clearly more than the president operating alone from a presidential vantage point. Results stem from a communal effort requiring that an indentifiable set of resources be employed in an undefinable set of ways. Some amount of success is highly likely, but as the product of a system geared to limited advocacy, no president can organize or influence others to follow his way all the time. So it is with presidential power. And so it is with the American democratic experiment.

POSTSCRIPT

Applying the Model: The Bush Drug Plan

As the Bush administration cleared the one year marker, scholars and journalists alike contended that the forty-first president spent much of his time handling foreign policy matters, to the exclusion of his domestic agenda. Breathtaking changes in Eastern Europe and the Soviet Union and the drug trade in Latin America dominated the president's attention, while he pursued a cautious "stay the course" approach on the home front, offering little in the way of new domestic initiatives. As the decade of the 1990s began, this combination seemed to play well with the public, as Bush was the recipient of unprecedented popular support.

I had intended to draw on a major Bush domestic policy case in an effort to apply the model developed in the first eight chapters to the current White House occupant. Yet, in his first year in office, George Bush provided a limited variety of items from which to select. The desire to use power to effect the direction of domestic policy is a central assumption of the model; to find a modern-day president who is not inclined to make an imprint on national domestic life is surprising indeed. Yet, in his first year, George Bush proved to be just that kind of chief executive, leaving us in the ironic and unexpected position of having to wait until the president *does* something before the findings discussed here can be applied.

Given the limited number of possibilities, I settled on what was perhaps the most hyped domestic initiative of the first year—the war on drugs—as a case that should fill in the general outlines of the way power has been exercised in the Bush White House. The president officially began work on his drug war in early September 1989, when his proposal was sent to Congress for scrutiny. Most of the action followed in the next few weeks, as congressional and

White House negotiators met to hammer out compromises on the president's proposal. One of the major stumbling blocks turned out to be funding for the drug war, and the president found himself temporarily faced with a confrontation between his stated desire to wage war against illegal drugs and his campaign pledge not to raise taxes.

During the negotiation period, the president held a "drug summit," created a White House Drug Advisory Council, and took his case to the public in personal meetings and on television. By early October, most of the behind-the-scenes work had been done, and the issue quickly faded from prominence. The result of the negotiating effort was a bill sent to the president on November 22, 1989, which approved small portions of the Bush drug measure. These included $180 million for the development of drug-free communities, $250 million for the expansion of rural substance abuse programs, and $125 million in foreign aid earmarked to combat cocaine production.

In a real sense, the major program that Bush proposed was quietly dropped from the agenda during negotiations. But, for what it became (more a skirmish against drugs than a full scale war), the president emerged from negotiations with something that represented a portion of his drug program. The results were not greeted with fanfare at the White House, and by all indications the president will reissue the call to arms in the future, aware that the drug fight has yet to be enjoined. But, for what he did accomplish, it is interesting to examine the state of the White House at the time and the impact it might have had on the outcome the president achieved. Most helpful to Bush were the White House organization, which was carefully constructed and efficiently run, and the economic climate, which supported rather than hindered the president's efforts. Less helpful were the limited access Bush allowed to members of Congress and the inconsistent manner in which he bargained, which in comparison to previous presidential policy successes were unspectacular.

☆ ☆ ☆ ☆ ☆ ☆ ☆ ☆

On September 6, 1989, the president and his drug czar William Bennett announced that they were together on a strategy to fight the war on drugs, marking the first indication that the White

House was organized for battle.[1] With only a couple of exceptions, the Bush White House was able to maintain a consistent level of efficiency throughout the next three months, most notably in its ability to remain internally coordinated around its plans for the drug program. For instance, six days later, after the president criticized congressional Democrats for focusing on higher taxes in order to combat drugs, his advisors "lined up vocally behind him, with Defense Secretary Dick Cheney protesting [Senator] Byrd's idea of reducing the Pentagon budget by $1.8 billion and national drug policy director William Bennett saying Bush's money request was adequate."[2]

Later that week, Bennett and his deputies specifically refused to be drawn into criticism of the Bush proposal. In early October, FBI director William Sessions and DEA administrator John Lawn resisted the same fate during testimony to Congress on the developing antidrug legislation.[3]

Lapses in coordination were the exception rather than the rule. A relatively minor one occurred toward the start of the campaign, when Bennett and one of his deputies disagreed on the role the military should play in the drug plan.[4] More significant was Bennett's criticism of governors attending President Bush's drug summit in late September, and the pursuant criticism of Bennett by White House chief of staff John Sununu. Bennett had said of the drug meetings: "There was standard Democratic pap. There was standard Republican pap, and there was stuff that rhymes with pap on both sides, too."[5] Sununu's response, that Bennett's remarks "weren't helpful,"[6] indicates in muted tones the degree of displeasure exhibited by the chief of staff over the departure from White House unity. But such lack of coordination among the ranks was the exception during the three months of the drug campaign, rather than the rule.

The reason for the high degree of coordination is in part the purposeful effort by the president to bring on board aides who naturally subscribed to his philosophy of and approach to government, among whom there would be little disagreement and, as such, minimal conflict. During the last few months of 1989, his efforts appeared to have been effective, as presidential surrogates successfully eschewed both policy *and* political differences. Writes one close observer: "So far, the Bush White House has been fairly calm without the backbiting and turf wars that were so prevalent in previous administrations. The president had one main criteria. He wanted people around him with whom he was comfortable and apparently he has lined up that kind of a team."[7]

Consistent with this observation is a fair amount of easy access among the principals developing the Bush plan, as well as between key White House players and the president. Generally speaking, Bennett and Sununu communicated freely with one another and with President Bush, as the White House operated on a direct access basis. And, there are indications that others in the White House by late September had come to see Sununu as a good man for the chief of staff position, "winning praise" from those around him for being "a quick study": "Presidential staffers say that the former New Hampshire governor has picked up fast on the 'byways of Capitol Hill' and the art of staying alive in big league politics."[8] Coupled with extensive coordination and low conflict surrounding the politics or policy of the drug plan, punctuated by few deviations from collective behavior, the Bush White House during the last few months of 1989 was an efficiently run place, rivaling in its own way the Reagan experience of early 1981.

Consider the data in Table P.1. Allowing for the small number of observations associated with the Bush administration, close to four in five references to organization capture the efficient manner in which the White House was operating as it worked on developing an antidrug program during the last three months of 1989. This ratio is identical to the figure realized by Bush's predecessor during his policy successes, and quite comparable to the 77 percent figure associated with policy success across the thirty-four cases

Table P.1. Values for Key Resources Used during the 1989 Bush "War on Drugs," in Relation to Comparable Values from Other Policy Cases

Resource	Value (N)	Comparison Value	Bush Resource Relative to Comparison Value
Organization	.79 (14)	Reagan Success, .79	Identical
Access	.78 (18)	All Failures, .72	Comparable
Persuasion	.65 (26)	All Failures, .56	Somewhat Higher
Bargaining	.55 (20)	Carter Failures, .42	Somewhat Higher

examined. In terms of its ability to function collectively, the Bush organization appears to have geared up for the drug campaign in a manner that mirrors the pattern evident in other recent administrations at times when they realized their policy goals. Taken alone, this observation suggests that the Bush administration faced Congress from a position of strength.

However, organization alone cannot ensure favorable outcomes, and beyond maintaining an efficient White House, the evidence that the Bush administration has optimized its power resources is mixed at best. Take the case of presidential and staff access to other policy players. During the brief period examined here, Bush and his surrogates in the aggregate were less accessible to Congress than some of his predecessors during their successful policy pursuits. In fact, where the Bush organization resembles the effective operation often associated with policy success, patterns of access fall short of the overwhelming openness also associated with successful outcomes.

As with most cases examined here, access was perceived to be present far more often than it was believed to be absent. Many of these references are to routine briefings or appearances by administration officials before congressional committees, such as when the president met with Republican congressional leaders on September 26 to discuss the drug plan or when Bennett testified to Congress shortly after the plan was announced that Bush had made the matter of illegal drugs "the centerpiece of his domestic agenda."[9]

At times, more extraordinary openness was evident. This was especially the case during a key marathon negotiating session held on September 22, during which Senate Minority Leader Robert Dole and other prominent Senate figures met for over seven hours with Bennett and budget director Richard Darmon to try to hammer out a compromise on the drug issue. During the meeting, Sununu remained in constant touch by phone, and Bush maintained open access to Sununu, thereby indirectly participating in the proceedings. Yet, there were also times when the president purposely held back from direct involvement. Consistent with his well-documented cautious nature, Bush would repeatedly keep his distance from the specific maneuvering taking place over the drug plan, at times refusing to meet with members of Congress and on rare occasions refusing to encounter his own people about particular issues, as when he refused to meet with Bennett to discuss his controversial comments about the Bush education summit. The overall effect of this distance is evident in the fact that the proportion of comments mentioning that access was granted (.78) is far lower than that achieved by other presidents who had an organization that ran as efficiently as the Bush White House.

It is not clear at this stage if the occasional Bush reluctance to jump into the fray and make himself widely accessible during policy negotiations will hamper him in the long run. In 1989, it did not appear to hurt him with the drug package, but of course the meaty core of the package still remained on the table even after the president's limited success of November 22. In a more complex, urgent, or contentious political climate, the president's caution may be less well suited to effecting the outcomes he seeks than it was in 1989. Such appears to have been the case during the troubled budget negotiations of October 1990, when a reluctant George Bush exacerbated a difficult situation by his uneven participation. As long as he maintains the organization he has built, Bush should have the tools necessary to effect access with others; beyond this, whether he is so inclined to use them is a matter of his political approach and personal style of governing.

The same may be said of bargaining. As with access, the president has built an organization that may serve as a vantage point from which effective bargaining may follow. But, the limited data available from the final months of 1989 indicate that President Bush was tentative when it came to bargaining in general and persuasion in particular. Only slightly better than half the references to bargaining incorporated mentions of the president's use of bargaining resources. Of those bargaining resources designed to persuade—favors, personal flexibility, and rapport—only about two in three references indicated they were put into action. Both figures are but slightly higher than those realized by President Carter during his unsuccessful efforts to institute a comprehensive energy program and eliminate select water resource projects during the early days of his administration.

Part of the problem stems from a tendency on the part of the president to remain inflexible in the eyes of other policy actors, even as he contends that he is open to compromise. A case in point occurred early in the drug negotiations, during which time the public words and private actions of the president were at odds with one another. In public, Bush insisted that he was willing to negotiate with congressional Democrats over specifics of the drug policy. At the time, the foremost Democratic proposal on funding had been offered by Senator Byrd—a proposal the president said he would veto. Several times during the week of September 10, Bush argued that his veto position was a no-compromise stand.[10] When an alternative proposal was submitted as a compromise measure by Senator Fritz Hollings, the president's stand was initially as staunch. Only in time, and "reluctantly," did the president come around to accept the Hollings compromise (a proposal that was eventually rejected by Senate Democrats). One day later, the president again insisted that he had been "very flexible" over the issue of how to fund the drug war.[11]

On other occasions, Bush has contended that he prefers to cooperate, and that he does not consider himself to be a confrontational president. His actions, as perceived by others in Washington, suggest this to be only partly true. Several times during the brief period covered by the drug case, Bush threatened to veto particular proposals, or, as was the case on November 7, to veto the entire bill if necessary. The flexibility he demonstrated at particular times during the negotiations was tempered by his reluctance to compromise at others. Overall, Bush faced Congress with a mixed bag of behaviors, and a clear picture of Bush the bargainer has yet to emerge. But, my sense is that his initial reluctance to bargain may give way to greater flexibility when he believes a real compromise is possible. In this respect, Bush may prove to be more pragmatic than his immediate predecessor, who could be immovable on items that threatened fundamental ideological premises.

It may yet be the case that the president can be persuasive in a pinch, when something important is on the line. This appeared to occur in early 1990, when Congress threatened to override his veto of legislation permitting Chinese students residing in America to remain in this country. During a brief campaign characterized by intense activity, Bush appeared willing to use favors and pressure tactics to line up enough senators to avoid a likely override. Data are not available from this episode which, in keeping with the primary focus of the first Bush year, is foreign policy oriented. But, it may be an indication that should an important domestic matter emerge, Bush will not be reluctant to engage in a more aggressive persuasion campaign than was evident during the last days of 1989.

As the politics of the drug program were playing out, Bush benefited from economic conditions that remained favorable. The unemployment rate was stable at an average of 5.3 percent for the period, and consumer prices were rising at an annual rate of under 5 percent. This compares quite well with the economic conditions facing both Carter and Reagan during their respective first years in office. It indicates a favorable climate in which the president could work and increases the likelihood that effective use of presidential power resources could generate favorable policy outcomes.

Taken collectively, the evidence suggests that Bush was operating from a position of strength at the end of his first year in office, in which the probability was good that he could realize his domestic policy endeavors.[12] Economic circumstances were favorable, and his organization by all appearances was sound, mirroring the results of purposeful efforts at organization building that were well conceived and effectively executed. And, in fact, the president did realize a limited version of the drug package he submitted to Congress before the legislature adjourned for the year.

Lacking in the drug effort were overwhelming presidential access to Congress characteristic of previous presidential successes, and consistent presidential efforts at persuading by bargaining. These deficiencies are true to the Bush style, which is deliberately cautious and reserved. They may cause problems for the president, especially if a bolder drug plan hits the agenda in the future, or if the president finds himself in a battle over the budget of the sort that was emerging as of this writing, in which he needs to draw on his personal resources of persuasion. Or, he may learn from his 1989 experience (as his behavior in the wake of the China veto appears to suggest) and be more assertive in the future. As of this writing, President Bush maintains a bare domestic agenda. It is in this respect too soon to draw definitive conclusions about his current chances for the effective use of power in an arena in which his immediate predecessors were eager to fight, but in which the forty-first president appears more content to sit in the bleachers.

APPENDIX A

Intercoder Reliability

In an effort to verify the reliability of the coding method, two coders replicated the collection effort for a random sample of articles used in the study. It was expected that this effort would yield moderate to low coefficients of reproducibility. The coders came into the project untrained and had to work with ambiguous data that demanded a high degree of judgment to decipher. Given limited resources, the effort to train the coders was restricted to six practice articles and personal discussion about the instruction booklet provided to each coder prior to the start of work. The categories were fixed before hand. Thus, there was little the researcher could do to enhance reliability, and little reason to expect high levels of agreement.[1]

Given this background, the results are especially impressive. The primary task was to record whether each resource was mentioned in a given article. The coders worked independently with the same coding sheet used by the researcher, and their findings were compared line by line for each article. For each resource in each article, any match between coder and researcher on the presence or absence of the resource is coded as an agreement. The ratio of total agreements to total possible resource mentions composes the measure of resource agreement reported in Table A.1. Total agreement is both consistent and high between each coder and the researcher and between the two coders (intercoder).

For each "matched" resource, agreement between coder and researcher was evaluated for other key variables used in the study. These include whether the resource was "used" or "not

Table A.1. Coding Agreement: Resource Variable

	Coder A	Coder B	Intercoder
Resource Agreement	.90	.84	.89

used'' by the president, mentions of policy actors (usually in Congress or the executive branch) who were the recipients of presidential resources, and references to the effectiveness of given resources as measured on a 5-point scale. In each case, agreement constituted exact replication of the way the item was coded by the researcher. The results appear in Table A.2.

The used-not used variable is highly reliable, no doubt because it is dichotomous and because clear and simple decision rules dictate its use. The actors variable, for which four choices are available on the code sheet, multiple mentions are possible, and ''other'' mentions are determined at the discretion of the coder, bears measures of agreement that are less striking but consistent and strong. A more tempered statement may be made about the effectiveness variable.

Admittedly, coding the effectiveness variable involves judgment and careful reading; it is assumed to be susceptible *both* to differences of judgment between coders that might raise questions about reliability and to errors stemming from the lack of experience of the coders. Unfortunately, it is not possible to distinguish between these two or to estimate how much more agreement would occur with more coder training. However, it is possible to determine the percentage of errors attributable to coder disagreement over the most difficult task of placing items precisely on the scale. Maximum discretion was needed to make the subtle distinction between extreme and moderate values of effectiveness and between extreme and moderate values of ineffectiveness. To decipher how much coder error stemmed from these decisions, two sets of figures are presented denoting agreement based on both the original 5-point scale and on a 3-point adaptation that considered direction (effective, neutral, or ineffective) but not degree.

Table A.2. Coding Agreement: Four Variables, Plus Overall Agreement

	Coder A	Coder B	Intercoder
Used-Not Used	.96	.98	1.00
Actors	.77	.75	.73
Effectiveness (5-point)	.78	.66	.67
Effectiveness (3-point)	.81	.73	.77
Total Agreement	.86	.86	.86

Finally, agreement by resource was examined to determine if a particular resource was more difficult than any other to identify. The results may be found in Table A.3.

Table A.3. Coding Agreement: Specific Resources

	Coder A	Coder B	Intercoder
Personal Access	.90	.93	1.00
Staff Access	.86	.75	.88
Organizational Efficiency	.86	.83	1.00
Pressure	.86	.89	.88
Threats	.89	.86	.88
Sanctions	1.00	1.00	1.00
Flexibility	.93	.93	.88
Rapport	.86	.96	.75
Favors	.96	.86	.88
Charm	1.00	.96	1.00
Information	.68	.93	.75
Expertise	.93	.96	1.00
Time	.86	.87	.75
Energy	.96	.96	1.00

APPENDIX B

Coding

The coding scheme employed here gleaned mentions of presidential resources from stories about each domestic policy case examined. Every story pertaining to each case was analyzed. To be included in the dataset, a reference to a resource needed to be unambiguous and attributed to a source. It also had to be connected to the case at hand; that is, resources used by the president for any purpose other than advancing the policy in question were omitted from consideration.

Resource mentions were often buried within stories. In example one, the reference to President Reagan telephoning undecided members of Congress is unambiguous, is attributed (to the president), and is connected to his effort to win approval of his budget proposal. Telephone conversations with members of Congress fall under the domain of personal access, so this reference was coded as the "use" of personal access. The story goes on to convey that the president tried to "enlist" congressional support, which is coded as a reference to the use of presidential pressure. The coding scheme does not discriminate among the many different types of pressure that may be applied by the president; "enlisting support," "twisting arms," and direct references to "pressing" or "using pressure" are coded the same way.

Example two is more complex. Note the uncoded reference to tempting senators with favors that occurs in the first paragraph. This is a *potential* event, as evidenced by the tense of the text ("The antitreaty side fears most that the administration *will* tempt"). It was not included among the data, as only observations of events that happened were coded. In fact, later in the text, Senator Zorinsky is quoted as observing that the administration was *not* trading favors. This is a reference to the failure to use a resource and is coded accordingly. Note also that an unrelated resource mention occurs in paragraph two (the use of staff access, as noted by Robert Strauss's comment about meeting with senators). Both resource mentions appearing in this story are attributed, but to different sources. One relates to the use of a resource, the other, to the failure to use a different resource. This is quite typical of the manner in which resource mentions appear in the printed record.

EXAMPLE ONE

"Reagan Resumes His Efforts On Economic Matters"
—*New York Times* (April 17, 1981), p. 8

President Reagan began preparations today to rejoin the fight to win congressional passage for his economic recovery program.

Mr. Reagan's top advisers have said that the effort to get the legislation passed had lagged during his convalescence from a gunshot wound suffered in an assassination attempt. Today, for the first time since he was shot on March 30, *Mr. Reagan telephoned several undecided congressmen* to try *to enlist their support,* according to Larry Speakes, the deputy White House press secretary.

Code: Personal access (used)
Pressure (used)

EXAMPLE TWO

"Canal Holdouts Find Pressure Mounting"
—*New York Times* (March 10, 1978), p. A6

The antitreaty side fears most that the administration will tempt the uncommitted senators with such bait as dams or judgeships or contracts, according to Senator Paul Laxalt, Republican of Nevada, a leading opponent.

But Robert S. Strauss, President Carter's trade negotiator who, as former Chairman of the Democratic National Committee, would be just the person who would handle that type of persuasion said, *"I guess I've talked very seriously with 10 or 12 senators* I know well and the question of a quid pro quo has never been suggested.

That was also the word from the State Department and the White House, and from uncommitted senators. *Senator Zorinsky, a Nebraska Democrat, observed with a chuckle that while the administration had avoided such matters,* his constituents kept asking him, "why don't you trade for something for Nebraska?"

Code: Staff access (used)
Favors (not used)

APPENDIX C

Cases of Success and Failure

Table C.1. Policy Successes

Policy Success	Year	President
Tax Hike	1982	Reagan
Budget	1981	Reagan
Panama Canal Ratification	1978	Carter
Natural Gas Deregulation	1978	Carter
Rural Development	1972	Nixon
Product Safety	1972	Nixon
Food Stamps	1970	Nixon
Scenic Rivers	1968	Johnson
Wiretapping	1968	Johnson
Air Pollution Control	1967	Johnson
Social Security Hike	1967	Johnson
Health Care	1967	Johnson
Unemployment Funding	1965	Johnson
Immigration	1965	Johnson
Housing	1965	Johnson
Secondary Education	1965	Johnson
Appalachia Program	1965	Johnson

Table C.2. Policy Failures

Policy Failure	Year	President
MX/Dense Pack	1982	Reagan
Hold Line on Taxes	1982	Reagan
Energy Program	1977	Carter
Eliminate Water Projects	1977	Carter
BEOG Grant	1976	Ford
Nuclear Power	1974	Nixon
Private School Tax Credit	1973	Nixon
Community Development	1973	Nixon
Mass Transit	1972	Nixon
Water Pollution	1972	Nixon
Milk Program	1970	Nixon
SST Funding	1970	Nixon
Social Security Hike	1970	Nixon
Consumer Protection	1970	Nixon
Air Pollution Control	1968	Johnson
Consumer Protection	1967	Johnson
Electoral College Reform	1966	Johnson

NOTES

INTRODUCTION

1. Alexander Passerin D'Entreves, *The Notion of the State* (London: Oxford University Press, 1967), p. 11.
2. Robert Dahl, "The Concept of Power," *Behavioral Science* 2 (July 1957): 201–215.
3. Passerin D'Entreves, *Notion of the State*, p. 11.
4. Edwards S. Corwin, *The President: Office and Powers* (New York: New York University Press, 1957).
5. Myron Q. Hale, "Presidential Influence, Authority, and Power and Economic Policy," in Dalmas H. Nelson and Richard L. Sklar, eds., *Towards a Humanistic Science of Politics* (New York: Latham, 1983), pp. 399–437.
6. Ibid.
7. The list is long and varied. For a discussion, see Robert E. Denton, "A Communication Model of Presidential Power," *Presidential Studies Quarterly* 18 (Summer 1988): 523–539.
8. Richard E. Neustadt, *Presidential Power: The Politics of Leadership from FDR to Carter* (New York: Macmillan Publishing, revised 1986).
9. Hale, "Presidential Influence," p. 408.
10. For a thoughtful discussion of the tendency for conventional presidential studies to gloss over objectives, see William F. Grover, *The President as Prisoner: A Structural Critique of the Carter and Reagan Years* (Albany: SUNY Press, 1989), p. 73 ff. Grover writes, "conventional accounts of the presidency stress means over, and almost to the exclusion of, ends. They view the office instrumentally, focusing on how to make it 'work better,' instead of investigating the fundamental reasons why it works the way it does, and subjecting the goals of the presidency to rigorous inquiry."

11. Gary King and Lyn Ragsdale, *The Elusive Executive* (Washington, DC: CQ Press, 1988), pp. 484–485.

CHAPTER I. THE PRESIDENT AND THE RABBIT

1. *New York Times* (August 30, 1979), p. 16.
2. Ibid.
3. For those interested in more details, and for those who wish to improve their Monopoly game, see Maxine Brady, *The Monopoly Book* (New York: David McKay Company, 1974).
4. See, for instance, Corwin, *The President;* Ferdinand Lundberg, *Cracks in the Constitution* (Secaucus, NJ: Lyle Stuart, 1980); or Richard M. Pious, *The American Presidency* (New York: Basic Books, 1979).
5. Neustadt, *Presidential Power.*
6. Actually, the two schools of thought need not be seen as mutually exclusive. Efforts have been made to combine them, for instance, by examining how the president uses available institutional forces to his advantage, and by considering how the competing models best fit different presidential roles. See David G. Wegge, "Neustadt's *Presidential Power:* The Test of Time and Empirical Research on the Presidency," *Presidential Studies Quarterly* 11 (Summer 1981): 342–347; and Raymond Tatalovich and Byron W. Daynes, "Toward A Paradigm to Explain Presidential Power," *Presidential Studies Quarterly* 9 (Fall 1979): 428–441.
7. This is barely the beginning of Dahl's treatise on power. For a more complete understanding of the concept of power as Dahl explains it, please see Robert Dahl, "The Concept of Power," *Behavioral Science* 2 (July 1957): 201–215. Social exchange theorists have employed a similar model to understand why individuals voluntarily maintain ongoing interactions with others in large social groups. See Peter Blau, *Exchanges and Power in Social Life* (New York: John Wiley and Sons, 1964); as well as George C. Homans, "Social Behavior as Exchange," in Edwin P. Hollander and Raymond G. Hunt, *Current Perspectives in Social Psychology: Readings With Commentary,* 2d ed. (New York: Oxford University Press, 1967), pp. 447–

458; and Elaine Hatfield Walster et al., *Equity: Theory and Research* (Boston: Allyn and Bacon, 1978).

8. Scholars have utilized the concept of resources to study a host of issues relating to the presidency. Dahl writes of patronage, influence, and charm in his analysis of power. Others discuss resources that will be addressed in the pages ahead. For example, see Bert A. Rockman, *The Leadership Question: The Presidency and the American System* (New York: Praeger Publishers, 1984); Paul C. Light, *The President's Agenda: Domestic Policy Choice from Kennedy to Carter* (Baltimore: Johns Hopkins University Press, 1982); Richard P. Nathan, *The Administrative Presidency* (New York: John Wiley and Sons, 1983); and John F. Manley, "Presidential Power and White House lobbying," *Political Science Quarterly* 93 (Summer 1978): 255–275.

9. Dahl, "The Concept of Power."

10. Neustadt, *Presidential Power,* p. 16, emphasis in original.

11. As a seminal work on the subject, *Presidential Power* has inspired scholars to explore and apply Neustadt's findings, as well as to question his method and approach. For applications of Neustadt's work, see George C. Edwards, *Presidential Influence in Congress* (San Francisco: W. H. Freeman and Company, 1980) and Manley, "Presidential Power and White House Lobbying." For criticism of Neustadt, see Thomas E. Cronin, "Presidential Power Reviewed and Reappraised," *Western Political Quarterly* 32 (December 1979): 381–395; John Hart, "Presidential Power Revisited," *Political Studies* 25 (March 1977): 48–61; and Peter Sperlich, "Bargaining and Overload: An Essay on Presidential Power," in Aaron Wildavsky, ed., *Perspectives on the Presidency* (Boston: Little, Brown and Company, 1975), pp. 406–430.

12. Two good critiques of this point may be found in Hart, "Presidential Power Revisited," and Cronin, "Presidential Prower Reviewed and Reappraised."

13. Foreign policy initiatives were excluded from analysis to narrow the focus of an admittedly broad study and because of unanswered questions about whether the exercise of presidential power is conceptually different in the foreign policy domain. See Aaron Wildavsky, "The Two Presidencies," in Wildavsky, ed., *Perspectives on the Presidency,* as well as Frederick P. Lee, "The Two Presidencies Revisited," *Presidential Studies Quarterly* 10 (Fall 1980): 620–628; Lee Sigelman, "A Reassessment of the Two Presidencies Thesis," *Journal*

of Politics 41 (November 1979): 1195–1205; and Donald Peppers, "The Two Presidencies: Eight Years Later," in Wildavsky, ed., *Perspectives on the Presidency,* pp. 462–470.

CHAPTER 2. POLICY OUTCOMES: POWER AND CONTEXT

1. David R. Gergen, "Can We Have An Effective Presidency?" *Presidential Studies Quarterly* 18 (Summer 1988): 475–483.

2. One may question the relationship between observations about the president that appear in print and the outcome of a particular case. If the president appears to be succeeding, could this not cast a halo over coverage and bias the manner in which his actions are reported? This needs to be considered as a possible source of error. However, there is reason to believe that the effect may be minimal. Many cases progress unevenly from start to finish, their outcomes unclear for long periods of time. Observations garnered from stories written during such periods of ambiguity would be untouched by this halo effect. Furthermore, one of the eight primary cases—Jimmy Carter's successful effort to win ratification of the Panama Canal treaties—quite literally came down to the wire. No one in Washington, including reporters, knew whether Carter would succeed until the Senate voted. Key data from this case compare quite favorably with data from other policy "successes," suggesting limitations to the extent that coverage of presidential behavior during policy success is a function of the fact that reporters perceive the president to be succeeding.

3. Supplementary data were gathered only from the *New York Times* and major periodicals, as the primary coding effort revealed a high rate of overlap among media.

4. The universe was compiled from major domestic policy items listed among the *Congressional Quarterly* presidential and congressional boxscores for the years 1964 through 1975. The presence of an item in the congressional boxscore was an indication of salience. The presidential boxscore, for the years it was published, contributed an assessment of the outcome (whether it was a success or failure) and indicated whether or not the initiative had active presidential backing. The 26 cases used represent 23 percent of the universe of 113 cases.

5. The requirement of salience is an important one, as it makes possible the distinction between domestic policy cases in which the president makes an effort to win support and those in which he merely goes through the motions. This concern is similar to one raised by Edwards about the use of presidential "support scores" as an indicator of presidential influence. Edwards aptly notes that support scores do not differentiate between active presidential support and limited or nonexistent presidential support for legislation. See George Edwards III, "Measuring Presidential Success in Congress: Alternative Approaches," *Journal of Politics* 47 (May 1985): 677–685.

6. *New York Times* (March 11, 1977), p. 27

7. Responses to the Gallup Poll question, "Do you approve or disapprove of the way Jimmy Carter is handling his job as President?"

8. *New York Times* (June 12, 1977), p. 26.

9. Ibid.

10. CBS Evening News/New York Times poll (September 1, 1977).

11. *New York Times* (September 27, 1977), p. 1.

12. Ibid. (September 26, 1977), p. 1.

13. Ibid. (October 6, 1977), Section IV, p. 1.

14. "CBS Evening News" (December 12, 1977), Walter Cronkite reporting.

15. *New York Times* (December 16, 1977), p. 28.

16. Ibid. (January 30, 1981), p. 1.

17. Pfiffner nicely documents how such efforts began long before the president took office. See James P. Pfiffner, "The Carter-Reagan Transition: Hitting the Ground Running," *Presidential Studies Quarterly* 13 (Fall 1983): 623–645.

18. *Washington Post* (February 20, 1981), p. 1.

19. *New York Times* (June 17, 1981), p. 1.

20. *Time* (August 10, 1981), p. 12.

21. Gallup poll (September 6, 1981).

22. For a good discussion, see Barbara Kellerman, *The Political Presidency: Practice of Leadership* (New York: Oxford University Press, 1984), pp. 185–253.

23. For a good review and analysis of this phenomenon, see Samuel Kernell, "Explaining Presidential Popularity," *American Political Science Review* 72 (June 1978): 506–522.

24. The figures here are from the Gallup poll.

25. In fact, the literature on this point is inconclusive, and the debate has a long history. Among those who feel public support is important to effective presidential leadership are Louis W. Koenig, *The Chief Executive* (New York: Harcourt, Brace, Jovanovich, 1975); Dorothy James, *The Contemporary Presidency* (New York: Pegasus Publishing, 1969); James Sundquist, *Politics and Policy* (Washington, DC: Brookings Institution, 1968); Wilfred E. Binkley, *President and Congress* (New York: Vintage Books, 1962); and Corwin, *The President*. For an alternative view, see Philippa Strum, *Presidential Power and American Democracy* (Pacific Palisades, CA: Goodyear Publishing Company, 1972); Grand McConnell, *The Modern Presidency* (New York: St. Martin's Press, 1967); and Elmer Cornwell, *Presidential Leadership of Public Opinion* (Bloomington: Indiana University Press, 1965).

26. Again, for a thorough analysis, see Kernell, "Explaining Presidential Popularity."

27. Rockman sees the give-and-take resulting from this struggle as a permanent part of the system, affecting the context in which presidents will try to lead. See Rockman, *The Leadership Question*.

28. *New York Times* (June 26, 1981), p. A14.

29. Specific references will be cited in subsequent passages, when the relationship of persuasion to power is discussed in full.

30. Light, *The President's Agenda,* pp. 177 – 178. Note that Light uses these terms in a different context.

31. The literature on LBJ is vast, and references to "the treatment" are numerous. For a personal account, see Hugh Sidey, *A Very Personal Presidency: Lyndon Johnson in the White House* (New York: Atheneum Publishers, 1968), pp. 70–82.

32. *New York Times* (May 10, 1981), Section IV, p. 18.

33. Ibid. (October 14, 1977), p. 17.

CHAPTER 3. BARGAINING AS PERSUASION

1. *Time* (April 25, 1977), p. 19.
2. Neustadt, *Presidential Power,* p. 45.
3. Please note that rapport is not charm. *Rapport* refers to the condition in effect between the president and other policy actors during acts of bargaining. *Charm* is a specific set of qualities that may or may not be held by the chief executive, which may contribute to the establishment of rapport.
4. *New York Times* (April 28, 1981), p. B14.
5. See, for instance, *US News and World Report* (June 1, 1981), p. 19.
6. *Newsweek* (March 8, 1982), p. 21.
7. *US News and World Report* (April 5, 1982), p. 23.
8. *Washington Post* (March 31, 1982), p. A25.
9. Ibid. (May 2, 1982). Although President Reagan briefly did engage in a dialogue with Congress about the tax issue, the talks were short-lived and collapsed partly under the weight of the president's refusal to compromise. In the wake of the failed talks, *US News and World Report* (May 10, 1982, p. 22) reported that an administration source insisted that "any concessions its side offered in the collapsed talks were no longer available," continuing the pattern of inflexibility that characterized the entire policy case.
10. *Newsweek* (April 4, 1977), p. 26.
11. *Washington Post* (March 16, 1977), p. A21.
12. Ibid. (May 28, 1977), p. A13.
13. Ibid. (April 23, 1977), p. 4.
14. *New York Times* (October 16, 1977), Section IV, p. 1.
15. *Newsweek* (October 10, 1977), p. 29.
16. *New York Times* (August 6, 1977), p. 1.
17. Ibid.
18. *Newsweek* (March 27, 1978), p. 42.
19. *Time* (April 24, 1978), p. 22.

20. *New York Times* (May 7, 1982), p. A1.

21. Ibid. (April 14, 1981), p. 1.

22. The scale captures the direction of the observation—whether favorable or unfavorable—and makes an attempt to capture intensity by identifying very favorable and very unfavorable comments based on the adjectives used. Favorable comments are recorded as positive integers (with *1* designated for favorable responses and *2* for very favorable responses); unfavorable responses are recorded as negative integers (with *−1* designated for unfavorable responses and *−2* for very unfavorable responses). Zero represents the neutral midpoint of the scale.

23. *New York Times* (May 8, 1981), p. A18.

24. Although 100 percent of the references to rapport occurring during Carter policy successes suggest that the president worked to generate good feeling, please note that this includes only five mentions of the resource.

25. Only two evaluations of rapport were available for Carter policy successes.

26. *Washington Post* (June 12, 1977), p. A11.

27. *New York Times Magazine* (July 24, 1977), p. 9.

28. *Time* (April 4, 1977), p. 16.

29. *Science* (June 17, 1977), p. 1304.

30. *New York Times Magazine* (July 24, 1977), p. 9.

31. Ibid.

32. *New York Times* (March 14, 1978), p. A7.

33. *Newsweek* (March 27, 1978), p. 42.

34. *New York Times* (March 14, 1978), p. A1.

35. *Time* (March 27, 1978), p. 10.

36. *Washington Post* (March 15, 1978), p. A11.

37. Ibid.

38. *New York Times* (April 28, 1981), p. B14.

39. Ibid. (May 1, 1981), p. A19.

40. *Washington Post* (August 20, 1982), p. A5.

41. *Time* (August 30, 1982), p. 16.

42. Ibid.

43. *Newsweek* (August 10, 1981), p. 17.

CHAPTER 4. DOMINATION AS PERSUASION

1. The number of references to pressure is far greater for both presidents during their policy triumphs, suggesting the possibility that the resource is used more extensively during successful pursuits. However, the varying length and intensity of the cases makes this possibility far from conclusive.

2. *New York Times* (April 21, 1981), p. B12.

3. *Newsweek* (August 15, 1977), p. 29.

4. *New York Times* (June 21, 1981), Section IV, p. 1.

5. Ibid. (April 16, 1981), p. A20.

6. Ibid. (April 21, 1981), p. B12.

7. Ibid. (April 28, 1981), p. B14.

8. Ibid. (September 1, 1977), p. A2.

9. Ibid. (November 18, 1977), p. A17.

10. Ibid. (January 17, 1978), p. A10.

11. *Washington Post* (March 19, 1978), p. A9.

12. *New York Times* (April 13, 1978), p. A1.

13. *US News and World Report* (April 24, 1978), p. 34. Note that such evaluations were not the exclusive province of policy failure.

14. *New York Times* (June 12, 1977), p. 26.

15. Ibid (May 27, 1977), p. A1.

16. Ibid.

17. Ibid. (October 7, 1977), p. 1.

CHAPTER 5. ORGANIZATIONAL EFFICIENCY

1. *New York Times* (August 1, 1977), p. 31.
2. *New York Times Magazine* (August 9, 1981), p. 31.
3. *Washington Post* (December 9, 1982), p. A11.
4. Mentions of the "White House" that could be taken to refer exclusively to the person of the president were excluded from analysis.
5. The additional cases were shorter in length and yielded fewer observations of organizational efficiency than the eight primary cases used in this study.
6. For discussions of presidential decision making and management in different policy arenas that treat the president's style as fixed, see Alexander George, *Presidential Decision-Making in Foreign Policy* (Boulder, CO: Westview Press, 1980); and Roger Porter, *Presidential Decision-Making: The Economic Policy Board* (New York: Cambridge University Press, 1980).
7. Fred Greenstein, *Leadership in the Modern Presidency* (Cambridge, MA: Harvard University Press, 1980), p. 351.
8. Ibid., p. 337.
9. For a review of some of the changes in the Carter White House following the president's first several months, see Eric L. Davis, "Legislative Liaison in the Carter Administration," *Political Science Quarterly* 94 (Summer 1979): 287–301.
10. See Joseph A. Pika, "Management Style and the Organizational Matrix," *Administration and Society* 20 (May 1988): 3–29. Pika distinguishes between "personalists," whose focus on management style stems from a perspective that sees White House staff as presidential extensions, and "institutionalists," who approach the institutional presidency as an entity with its own dynamics, separate from the president.
11. Greenstein, *Leadership in the Modern Presidency.*
12. See Pika, "Management Style and the Organizational Matrix."
13. See Rockman, *The Leadership Question;* and Charles O. Jones, "A New President, a Different Congress, a Maturing Agenda," in Lester M. Salamon and Michael S. Lund, eds., *The Reagan Presidency and*

the Governing of America (Washington, DC: Urban Institute Press, 1984), pp. 261–287.

14. Stephen Skowronek, "Presidential Leadership in Political Time," in Michael Nelson, ed., *The Presidency and the Political System* (Washington, DC: CQ Press, 1988), pp. 115–160.

15. Stephen J. Wayne, "Congressional Liaison in the Reagan White House: A Preliminary Assessment of the First Year," in Norman J. Ornstein, ed., *President and Congress: Assessing Reagan's First Year* (Washington, DC: American Enterprise Institute, 1982), p. 47.

16. Ibid., p. 49.

17. For an excellent account see Greenstein, *Leadership in the Modern Presidency.* See especially pp. 28–30 for an account of FDR's approach and pp. 85–88 for an account of Eisenhower.

18. Fred I. Greenstein, "Dwight D. Eisenhower: Leadership Theorist in the White House," in Greenstein, ibid., pp. 85–86.

19. Quoted in Light, *The President's Agenda,* p. 175.

20. Ibid., p. 179.

21. Ibid., p. 187.

22. John H. Kessel, "The Structures of the Carter White House," *American Journal of Political Science* 27 (August 1983): 439.

23. John H. Kessel, "The Structures of the Reagan White House," *American Journal of Political Science* 28 (May 1984): 231–258.

24. Many scholars have commented on this effort. See Hugh Heclo, "One Executive Branch or Many?" in Anthony King, ed., *Both Ends of the Avenue* (Washington, DC: AEI Press, 1983), pp. 26–57; Jones, "A New President, a Different Congress, a Maturing Agenda"; Chester A. Newland, "Executive Office Appointments: Enforcing the Reagan Agenda," in Salamon and Lund, *The Reagan Presidency and the Governing of America,* pp. 135–168; and Richard P. Nathan, "The Reagan Presidency in Domestic Affairs," in Fred I. Greenstein, ed., *The Reagan Presidency: An Early Assessment* (Baltimore: Johns Hopkins Press, 1983), pp. 48–81.

25. Nathan, "The Reagan Presidency in Domestic Affairs," p. 72.

26. In fact, Heclo ("One Executive Branch or Many?") points out that one major drawback of Reagan's approach was the inability to foster

continuity through the development of lasting relationships within the executive branch.

27. For an account of some important organizational changes in the Carter administration after the first six months, see Eric L. Davis, "Legislative Liaison in the Carter Administration," *Political Science Quarterly* 94 (Summer 1979): 287–301.

28. Heclo, "One Executive Branch or Many?"; Pika, "Management Style and the Organizational Matrix."

29. Heclo, ibid., p. 27.

30. *New York Times Magazine* (August 9, 1981), p. 31.

31. *New York Times* (June 26, 1981), p. A15.

32. Jones, "A New President, a Different Congress, a Maturing Agenda," p. 275.

33. Kessel, "The Structures of the Reagan White House."

34. Davis, "Legislative Liaison in the Carter Administration," p. 297.

35. *Time* (October 9, 1978), p. 23.

36. *New York Times* (August 29, 1977), p. A9.

37. Wayne, "Congressional Liaison in the Reagan White House," pp. 48–49.

38. *Newsweek* (May 27, 1978), p. 42.

39. Kessel, "The Structures of the Carter White House."

40. *Business Week* (November 14, 1977), p. 88.

41. Davis, "Legislative Liaison in the Carter Administration."

42. Ibid.; and Charles O. Jones, "Presidential Negotiation with Congress," in King, *Both Ends of the Avenue*, pp. 96–130.

43. *New York Times* (March 27, 1977), Section IV, p. 4.

44. *US News and World Report* (November 7, 1977), p. 21.

45. Light, *The President's Agenda*, pp. 229–230.

46. Wayne, "Congressional Liaison in the Reagan White House," p. 47.

47. Ibid.

48. Betty Glad, *Jimmy Carter* (New York: W. W. Norton and Company, 1980), p. 146.

49. Charles O. Jones, "Ronald Reagan and the US Congress: Visible-Hand Politics," in Jones, ed., *The Reagan Legacy: Promise and Performance* (Chatham, NJ: Chatham House Publishers, 1988), p. 35. See also Wayne, "Congressional Liaison in the Reagan White House," and Jones, "A New President, a Different Congress, a Maturing Agenda."

50. Wayne, ibid., pp. 49–50.

51. Jones, "Ronald Reagan and the US Congress."

52. Jones, "A New President, a Different Congress, a Maturing Agenda," p. 274.

53. Jones, "Ronald Reagan and the US Congress," pp. 35–36.

54. Heclo sees a similar phenomenon among the presidency, the federal bureaucracy, Congress, and the court system, given the growth of each institution and the concomitant tendency for all players to feel a reduced sense of common needs and interests.

55. Light, *The President's Agenda;* and Pika, "Management Style and the Organizational Matrix."

56. Light, ibid., p. 182.

57. Wayne, "Congressional Liaison in the Reagan White House," pp. 50–51.

58. *Time* (August 23, 1982), p. 8.

59. For a full comparison, see Kessel, "The Structures of the Carter White House," and "The Structures of the Reagan White House."

60. As his administration progressed, the inner circle gradually dissolved.

61. *Business Week* (November 14, 1977), p. 88.

62. *New York Times* (October 9, 1977), Section IV, p. 14.

63. Wayne, "Congressional Liaison in the Reagan White House," p. 48.

64. *Washington Post* (March 19, 1978), p. A7.

65. Light (*The President's Agenda*) addresses both of these aspects of presidential involvement. See especially pp. 154 and 183–185.

66. See Glad, *Jimmy Carter,* esp. p. 147.

67. Davis, "Legislative Liaison in the Carter Administration," p. 291.

68. Jones, "A New President, a Different Congress, a Maturing Agenda," p. 274.

69. *Time* (March 27, 1978), p. 13.

70. *Newsweek* (March 28, 1977), p. 17.

71. *New York Times* (August 2, 1977), p. 14.

72. Ibid. (October 14, 1977), p. 17.

73. *Time* (August 29, 1977), p. 28.

74. The reader will recall that the scale captures the direction of the observation — whether favorable or unfavorable — and makes an attempt to capture intensity by identifying very favorable and very unfavorable comments based on the adjectives used. Favorable comments are recorded as positive integers (with *1* designated for favorable responses and *2* for very favorable responses); unfavorable responses are recorded as negative integers (with *−1* designated for unfavorable responses and *−2* for very unfavorable responses). Zero represents the neutral midpoint of the scale.

75. Consider what Neustadt (*Presidential Power*) says about the damage this can do to the president's professional reputation.

CHAPTER 6. ACCESS AND OTHER RESOURCES

1. All references were attributed to a source and pertained directly to one of the policy cases. Passive references (such as "O'Neill had been briefed," when it was not known by whom, how, or when) were excluded.

2. Some references, such as those attributed to "the administration" or "the White House" could refer to the president or the president's staff or both.

3. *US News and World Report* (August 22, 1977), p. 26.

4. *New York Times* (September 1, 1977), p. A2.

5. *Washington Post* (October 12, 1977), p. A2.

6. Ibid. (August 19, 1978), p. A1.

7. Ibid. (September 1, 1978), p. A1.

8. *New York Times* (June 26, 1981), p. A14.

9. Jones, "Ronald Reagan and the US Congress," p. 34.

10. Wayne, "Congressional Liaison in the Reagan White House," p. 50.

11. *Business Week* (May 3, 1982), p. 28.

12. *New York Times* (May 30, 1982), Section IV, p. 4.

13. *Time* (August 23, 1982), p. 7.

14. *Newsweek* (August 23, 1982).

15. *New York Times* (February 13, 1977), Section IV, p. 1.

16. *Washington Post* (June 12, 1977), p. A11.

17. Light, *The President's Agenda,* p. 192.

18. Jones, "Ronald Reagan and the US Congress," p. 36. O'Neill goes on to say that he did not enjoy the same relationship with top Reagan aides later in the administration.

19. *New York Times* (April 1, 1977), p. 1.

20. Ibid. (February 3, 1977), p. 23.

21. Ibid. (April 24, 1977), p. A28.

22. Ibid., p. A1.

23. Ibid. (November 2, 1977), p. D1.

24. Ibid. (April 9, 1977), p. 25.

25. Ibid. (June 2, 1977), p. A13.

26. Only evaluations of personal or staff access clearly attributed to congressional actors were recorded. The reader will recall that the scale captures the direction of the observation—whether favorable or unfavorable—and makes an attempt to capture intensity by identifying very favorable and very unfavorable comments based on the adjectives used. Favorable comments are recorded as positive integers (with *1* designated for favorable responses and *2* for very favorable responses); unfavorable responses are recorded as negative integers (with *−1* designated for unfavorable responses and *−2* for very unfavorable responses). Zero represents the neutral midpoint of the scale.

27. Ibid. (February 5, 1981), p. 20.

28. *US News and World Report* (April 6, 1981), p. 28.

29. *New York Times* (July 30, 1981), p. D21.

30. *New York Times* (August 2, 1977), p. 14.

31. Ibid. (August 19, 1978), p. 22.

32. Ibid. (August 20, 1978), p. 9.

33. *US News and World Report* (August 30, 1982), p. 7.

34. For a discussion, see Dean Keith Simonton, *Why Presidents Succeed: A Political Psychology of Leadership* (New Haven, CT: Yale University Press, 1987).

35. Obviously, references to charm are not always articulated. We would expect that many such references would never find their way into print, and in fact the total number of observations is quite small. In this respect, the methodology used in this study is less suited to capture observations of this resource than others that attract more widespread comment. This is meant as an approximate measure, based on the number of publicly recorded observations of presidential charm attributed specifically to one of the policy cases under study.

36. *Washington Post* (April 8, 1981), p. A4.

37. *US News and World Report* (March 2, 1981), p. 28.

38. This is not meant in a pejorative sense, nor is it intended as a global evaluation of the president. Expertise is discussed from the narrow perspective of technical appreciation and understanding and does not address the president's ability to wield other resources or to use his political skills.

39. *New York Times* (April 1, 1977), p. 1.

40. Ibid. (March 18, 1977), p. 11.

41. *Newsweek* (August 10, 1981), p. 19.

42. *US News and World Report* (March 2, 1981), p. 28.

43. Ibid.

44. *Newsweek* (February 1, 1982), p. 16.

45. Ibid.

46. *New York Times* (February 3, 1977), p. 23.

47. Ibid. (April 24, 1977).

48. Ibid. (October 21, 1977), p. A12.

49. *Newsweek* (May 2, 1977), p. 16.

50. *US News and World Report* (September 12, 1977), p. 49.

51. *New York Times* (February 23, 1981), p. 1.

52. *US News and World Report* (March 23, 1981), p. 27.

53. *New York Times* (August 2, 1981), Section IV, p. 21.

54. *US News and World Report* (March 23, 1981), p. 27.

55. *New York Times* (August 20, 1982), p. D14.

56. *Time* (July 6, 1981), p. 7.

57. *Newsweek* (July 4, 1977), p. 49.

CHAPTER 7. POWER AND CONTEXT

1. *New York Times* (May 3, 1981), Section IV, p. 1.

2. This is essentially Neustadt's concept of public prestige, which he believes delimits the president's ability to exercise power. A president steeped in popular support is a president who has to be seriously regarded, unlike a president who generates doubt in the minds of voters, or who, like Nixon in 1974, has lost the support of the people.

3. Average presidential approval ratings for each policy case were calculated from all Gallup data collected during the period.

4. Measured as a "dummy" variable equal to *1* if a policy case occurred during the first six months of a new term, *0* otherwise.

5. Following Kernell, the number of battle deaths during the period of each policy case was used as an approximation of the war's intensity. Watergate was measured as a "dummy" variable, assumed to be "present" for all cases occurring from July 1972 through 1974.

6. See Kernell, "Explaining Presidential Popularity."

7. All but Watergate were significant when regressed on Gallup approval.

8. Given the relatively small number of cases available for analysis (N = 34), the number of variables that could be used in the model was necessarily limited. Both theoretical and methodological concerns influenced the selection of the variables discussed here.

9. In cases such as this one, ordinary least squares is not appropriate because some of the standard assumptions do not apply. Most important, because the observed value of Y for each event may be only 1 (if the event did occur) or 0 (if the event did not occur), the associated error term U_t may assume only two possible values: if $1 = X_tB + U_t$, $U_t = 1 - X_tB$; if $0 = X_tB + U_t$, $U_t = -X_tB$. If B is unbiased, $E(U_t) = \Sigma U_t f(U_t) = 0$, and the variance of $U_t = E(U_t^2) = \Sigma U_t^2 f(U_t)$, a quantity that will depend on the values of X_t. This violates the assumption of homoskedasticity, making OLS inappropriate. For a discussion, see Eric A. Hanushek and John E. Jackson, *Statistical Methods for Social Scientists* (New York: Academic Press, 1977), Chapter 7, and Alan Agresti, *Analysis of Ordinal Categorical Data* (New York: John Wiley and Sons, 1984).

10. Such as voting studies. See, for instance, Raymond E. Wolfinger and Steven J. Rosenstone, *Who Votes?* (New Haven, CT: Yale University Press, 1980).

11. Some cases lasted for months, but involved minor or sporadic resource activity. Others were brief but intensely fought battles. To control for the varying duration and intensity of the policy cases, values of the independent variables were weighted by an "intensity index," which is the ratio *Number of resource mentions/number of days*. The number of resource mentions is the total number of references to all resources coded for the case. The number of days is the period covered by the coding effort. For the sake of clarity, values used in the following discussion are not weighted.

12. That is to say, a value for Y is predicted for each case, given the estimates of the logit model. If $Y > .5$ when the true value of $Y = 1$ (i.e., a "success"), the model predicted correctly. Likewise, if the predicted value of $Y < .5$ when the true value of $Y = 0$ (i.e., a "failure"), the model also predicted correctly. Given the fact that the probability of success for the cases examined here, at the outset, is somewhat greater than chance, the results are particularly strong. Although the policy cases addressed here were randomly selected from among salient presidential initiatives, the initiatives themselves were likely pursued by presidents in part because they felt they had a fairly high probably of being realized. As a consequence, the universe and therefore the sample constitute cases with a probability for success greater than chance. We would expect the strong results witnessed here to be even stronger if this selection bias were not present.

13. The marginal impact of any exogenous variable on the likelihood of policy success may be determined by calculating the probability of success as $p = 1 / 1 + e^{(-X_i B)}$. By calculating p with different values for organizational efficiency, holding all other X values constant, it is possible to determine the effect on the probability attributable to different values of organization.

14. The probabilities are determined using weighted values for the explanatory variables. Unweighted values are used in the discussion.

15. The relationship between poor organization and restricted access is not a direct one in every case. Recall that access with Congress remained relatively high during President Reagan's failures, even though his organization suffered from inefficiency.

16. An interaction term was omitted from the model because the relatively small case size restricted the number of variables that could be included.

17. *Washington Post* (April 29, 1982), p. A1.

18. *New York Times* (June 28, 1981), Section IV, p. 4.

19. Ibid., p. A28.

20. Ibid. (July 30, 1981), p. D21.

21. *Washington Post* (May 22, 1981), p. A21.

22. *Newsweek* (March 27, 1978).

23. *New York Times* (March 15, 1978), p. A6.

24. Ibid. (March 17, 1978), p. A12.

25. For purposes of comparison, it is assumed that the duration and intensity of the two hypothetical cases are equal to the 1977 Carter energy drive.

POSTSCRIPT: APPLYING THE MODEL: THE BUSH DRUG PLAN

1. All references to the Bush drug plan contained in this postscript come from the United Press International Domestic News Wire or the UPI Political Wire.

2. UPI (September 12, 1989).
3. Ibid. (October 3, 1989).
4. Ibid. (September 11, 1989).
5. Ibid. (September 29, 1989).
6. Ibid.
7. Ibid. (September 28, 1989), Helen Thomas reporting.
8. Ibid.
9. Ibid. (September 7, 1989).
10. See especially UPI (September 12–14, 1989).
11. Ibid. (September 16, 1989).
12. Given the limited number of resource observations associated with the drug policy, I am reluctant to use the equation presented in the previous chapter to assess specific probability values for the likelihood of success.

APPENDIX A. INTERCODER RELIABILITY

1. See Oli Holsti, *Content Analysis for the Social Sciences* (Reading, MA: Addison-Wesley, 1969).

SELECT BIBLIOGRAPHY

Binkley, Wilfred E. *President and Congress*. New York: Vintage Books, 1962.

Blau, Peter. *Exchanges and Power in Social Life*. New York: John Wiley and Sons, 1964.

Cornwell, Elmer. *Presidential Leadership of Public Opinion*. Bloomington: Indiana University Press, 1965.

Corwin, Edwin S. *The President: Office and Powers*. New York: New York University Press, 1957.

Cronin, Thomas E. "Presidential Power Reviewed and Reappraised." *Western Political Quarterly* 32 (December 1979): 381–395.

Dahl, Robert. "The Concept of Power." *Behavioral Science* 2 (July 1957): 201–215.

Davis, Eric L. "Legislative Liaison in the Carter Administration." *Political Science Quarterly* 94 (Summer 1979): 287–301.

Denton, Robert E. "A Communication Model of Presidential Power." *Presidential Studies Quarterly* 18 (Summer 1988): 523–539.

Edwards, George C. "Measuring Success in Congress: Alternative Approaches." *Journal of Politics* 47 (May 1985): 677–685.

———. *Presidential Influence in Congress*. San Francisco: W. H. Freeman and Company, 1980.

George, Alexander. *Presidential Decision-Making in Foreign Policy*. Boulder, CO: Westview Press, 1980.

Gergen, David R. "Can We Have an Effective Presidency?" *Presidential Studies Quarterly* 18 (Summer 1988): 475–483.

Glad, Betty. *Jimmy Carter*. New York: W. W. Norton and Company, 1980.

Greenstein, Fred I. *Leadership in the Modern Presidency*. Cambridge, MA: Harvard University Press, 1988.

———. *The Reagan Presidency: An Early Assessment*. Baltimore: Johns Hopkins Press, 1983.

Grover, William F. *The President as Prisoner: A Structural Critique of the Carter and Reagan Years*. Albany: SUNY Press, 1989.

Hale, Myron Q. "Presidential Influence, Authority, and Power and Economic Policy." In *Towards a Humanistic Science of Politics*, ed. Dalmas H. Nelson and Richard L. Sklar, pp. 399–437. New York: Latham, 1983.

Hart, John. "Presidential Power Revisited." *Political Studies* 25 (March 1977): 48–61.

Heclo, Hugh. "One Executive or Many?" In *Both Ends of the Avenue*, ed. Anthony King, pp. 26–57. Washington, DC: AEI Press, 1983.

Henderson, Phillip G. *Managing the Presidency*. Boulder, CO: Westview Press, 1988.

Homans, George C. "Social Behavior As Exchange." In *Current Perspectives in Social Psychology: Readings with Commentary*, 2d ed., ed. Edwin P. Hollander and Raymond G. Hunt. New York: Oxford University Press, 1967.

James, Dorothy. *The Contemporary Presidency*. New York: Pegasus Publishing, 1969.

Jones, Charles O. "Ronald Reagan and the US Congress: Visible-Hand Politics." In *The Reagan Legacy: Promise and Performance*, ed. Charles O. Jones, pp. 30–59. Chatham, NJ: Chatham House Publishers, Inc., 1988.

———. "A New President, a Different Congress, a Maturing Agenda." In *The Reagan Presidency and the Governing of America*, ed. Lester M. Salamon and Michael S. Lund, pp. 261–287. Washington, DC: The Urban Institute Press, 1984.

———. "Presidential Negotiation with Congress." In *Both Ends of the Avenue*, ed. Anthony King, pp. 96–130. Washington, DC: AEI Press, 1983.

Kellerman, Barbara. *The Political Presidency: Practice of Leadership*. New York: Oxford University Press, 1984.

Kernell, Samuel. "Explaining Presidential Popularity." *American Political Science Review* 72 (June 1978): 506–522.

Kessel, John H. "The Structures of the Reagan White House." *American Journal of Political Science* 28 (May 1984): 231–258.

———. "The Structures of the Carter White House." *American Journal of Political Science* 27 (August 1983): 431–463.

Kiewiet, Roderick D., and Matthew D. McCubbins. "Presidential Influence on Congressional Appropriations Decisions." *American Journal of Political Science* 32 (August 1988): 713–736.

King, Gary, and Lyn Ragsdale. *The Elusive Executive*. Washington, DC: CQ Press, 1988.

Koenig, Louis W. *The Chief Executive*. New York: Harcourt, Brace, Jovanovich, 1975.

Lee, Frederick P. "The Two Presidencies Revisited." *Presidential Studies Quarterly* 10 (Fall 1980): 620–628.

Light, Paul C. *The President's Agenda: Domestic Policy Choice from Kennedy to Carter.* Baltimore: Johns Hopkins University Press, 1982.

Lundberg, Ferdinand. *Cracks in the Constitution*. Secaucus, NJ: Lyle Stuart, 1980.

Manley, John F. "Presidential Power and White House Lobbying." *Political Science Quarterly* 93 (Summer 1978): 255–275.

McConnell, Grant. *The Modern Presidency.* New York: St. Martin's Press, 1967.

Nathan, Richard P. *The Administrative Presidency.* New York: John Wiley and Sons, 1983.

———. "The Reagan Presidency In Domestic Affairs." In *The Reagan Presidency: An Early Assessment,* ed. Fred I. Greenstein, pp. 48–81. Baltimore: Johns Hopkins Press, 1983.

Neustadt, Richard E. *Presidential Power: The Politics of Leadership from FDR to Carter.* New York: Macmillan Publishing, 1986.

Newland, Chester A. "Executive Office Appointments: Enforcing the Reagan Agenda." In *The Reagan Presidency and the Governing of America,* ed. Lester M. Salamon and Michael S. Lund, pp. 135–168. Washington, DC: Urban Institute Press, 1984.

Passerin D'Entreves, Alexander. *The Notion of the State*. London: Oxford University Press, 1967.

Peppers, Donald. ''The Two Presidencies: Eight Years Later.'' In *Perspectives on the Presidency,* ed. Aaron Wildavsky, pp. 462–470. Boston: Little, Brown and Company, 1975.

Pfiffner, James P. ''The Carter-Reagan Transition: Hitting the Ground Running.'' *Presidential Studies Quarterly* 13 (Fall 1983): 623–645.

Pika, Joseph A. ''Management Style and the Organizational Matrix.'' *Administration and Society* 20 (May 1988): 3–29.

Pious, Richard M. *The American Presidency.* New York: Basic Books, 1979.

Porter, Roger. *Presidential Decision-Making: The Economic Policy Board.* New York: Cambridge University Press, 1980.

Rockman, Bert A. *The Leadership Question: The Presidency and the Amercian System.* New York: Praeger Publishers, 1984.

Sidey, Hugh. *A Very Personal Presidency: Lyndon Johnson in the White House.* New York: Atheneum Publishers, 1968.

Sigelman, Lee. ''A Reassessment of the Two Presidencies Thesis.'' *Journal of Politics* 41 (November 1979): 1195–1205.

Simonton, Dean Keith. *Why Presidents Succeed: A Political Psychology of Leadership.* New Haven, CT: Yale University Press, 1987.

Skowronek, Stephen. ''Presidential Leadership in Political Time.'' In *The Presidency and the Political System,* ed. Michael Nelson, pp. 115–160. Washington, DC: CQ Press, 1988.

Sperlich, Peter. ''Bargaining and Overload: An Essay on Presidential Power.'' In *Perspectives on the Presidency,* ed. Aaron Wildavsky, pp. 406–430. Boston: Little, Brown and Company, 1975.

Strum, Philippa. *Presidential Power and American Democracy.* Pacific Palisades, CA: Goodyear Publishing Company, 1972.

Sundquist, James. *Politics and Policy.* Washington, DC: Brookings Institution, 1968.

Walster, Elaine Hatfield, et al. *Equity: Theory and Research.* Boston: Allyn and Bacon, 1978.

Wayne, Stephen J. ''Congressional Liaison in the Reagan White House: A Preliminary Assessment of the First Year.'' In *President and Congress: Assessing Reagan's First Year,* ed. Norman J. Ornstein, pp. 44–65. Washington, DC: American Enterprise Institute, 1982.

Wildavsky, Aaron. "The Two Presidencies." In *Perspectives on the Presidency,* ed. Aaron Wildavsky. Boston: Little, Brown and Company, 1975.

Wolfinger, Raymond E., and Steven J. Rosenstone. *Who Votes?* New Haven, CT: Yale University Press, 1980.

INDEX